## About the Author

Theresa Cheung was born into a family of psychics and Spiritualists. Since gaining a Masters from King's College, Cambridge, she has been involved in the serious study of the paranormal for over 25 years and has been a student of the College of Psychic Studies in London. She is the author of a variety of books, including the international bestseller *The Element Encyclopedia of 20,000 Dreams* as well as *The Element Encyclopedia of the Psychic World*, *The Element Encyclopedia of Birthdays* and *Working with Your Sixth Sense* and *Working with Your Dreams*. Her books have been translated into 25 different languages and her writing has also featured in *It's Fate*, *Spirit and Destiny*, *High Spirit* and *Prediction* magazines. She has also worked on books for Derek Acorah, Yvette Fielding and Tony Stockwell.

Theresa believes this book and her two previous angel books, *The Sunday Times* bestselling *An Angel Called My Name* and *An Angel on My Shoulder*, were born in answer to her own questions and as a gift to herself and others. She has a great interest in angels, spirit guides, dreams and visions of the afterlife and feels that angels are directing her writing and her life. She has also had several angel experiences herself, some of which she shares here.

If you have had an angel experience and wish to share it with Theresa, she would love to hear from you. Please contact her care of HarperElement Editorial Department, 77–85 Fulham Palace Road, Hammersmith, London W6 8JB, or e-mail any inspiring and uplifting stories direct to her at: angeltalk710@aol.com.

# Angel Babies

# Angel Babies

And other true stories
of guardian angels

## Theresa Cheung

HarperElement
An Imprint of HarperCollins*Publishers*
77-85 Fulham Palace Road,
Hammersmith, London W6 8JB

The website address is: www.thorsonselement.com

and *HarperElement* are trademarks of
HarperCollins*Publishers* Ltd

First published by HarperElement 2009

3

A catalogue record of this book is
available from the British Library

ISBN 978-0-00-730996-2

Printed and bound in Great Britain by
Clays Ltd, St Ives plc

FSC is a non-profit international organization established to promote the
responsible management of the world's forests. Products carrying the FSC
label are independently certified to assure consumers that they come
from forests that are managed to meet the social, economic and
ecological needs of present and future generations.

Find out more about HarperCollins and the environment at
**www.harpercollins.co.uk/green**

# Contents

## Your Guardian Angel

You have a guardian angel
Who watches over you –
Everywhere you go
And everything you do.
This gentle, silent helper
Is there to be your guide
To shelter and protect you,
And for you to walk beside.
Your angel will always help you
Whenever things go wrong,
They'll be the wings beneath your feet
As life's path you walk along.
Feel this calming presence,
Be enfolded by its love,
And let your life be guided
By a power from above.

**Anonymous**

# Introduction: An Angel at my Door

'A house call from an angel can
heal a broken heart.'

**Anonymous**

Anyone who knows me or who has read my previous angel books, *An Angel Called My Name* or *An Angel on My Shoulder*, will know that without a shadow of doubt I believe in angels. I believe that departed loved ones watch over us from the other side and that each one of us has a guardian angel guiding us both in this life and the next.

I also believe that our guardian angels can manifest their loving presence in a limitless number of ways. On rare occasions they appear in their full-blown glory, complete with wings and halos, but more often than not they prefer to express themselves in subtler, gentler ways.

They may appear in our dreams, in a flash of insight, in a hug or in other people who are consciously or unconsciously guided by those in the world of spirit. They may manifest as a gentle breeze, a cloud, a bird, a coin, a song or anything that speaks volumes to our hearts. They may choose to express their love through the spirits of departed loved ones. Last, but by no means least, they may appear or express themselves through children or those with a youthful spirit. Indeed, the ability to live life with the open and trusting heart of a child may well be the vital ingredient angels need to manifest their loving presence on Earth.

In my previous angel books I gathered together collections of true-life angel stories from people of all ages and backgrounds, and it soon became clear to me that a great many of the stories focused on the experiences of the very young. Another theme I noticed was that regardless of their age, people who encountered angels or believed that angels were watching over them tended to be young in their approach to life. I've been researching and writing about angels and afterlife experiences for many years now and looking back I can see that almost from the very beginning this 'young at heart' theme was quite literally knocking on my door.

## Opening the Door

About a decade ago I was in the bathroom when a boy of about eight or nine rang my doorbell. He had my eight-month-old son in his arms. I was stunned, as I had left my son on the living-room rug for just a few moments and he was crawling but not yet walking.

The boy at my door told me he had found my baby crawling on our porch dangerously close to some steps which led down to a stone path. Wracked with shock, guilt and relief, I snatched my son and hugged him tightly to me, closing my eyes. Then I remembered the boy at the door and how abrupt I must have seemed. I hadn't even thanked him. I opened my eyes, intending to ask his name and give him some money, but he was nowhere to be seen. Holding my son tightly, I walked down the stairs and looked up and down the street outside our house. I was convinced I would see the boy walking away either to the left or to the right, as the street was straight and there were no bends or turnings he could head down, but there was no trace of him in either direction. He had vanished.

Whether human or in spirit, this boy will always be an angel in my eyes, as there is no telling what might have happened if my precious baby had fallen down those stairs. Even now, all these years later, I can still picture him in my mind, with his twinkling blue eyes, lopsided smile and mop of dark hair. Many people have told me that he was probably just a kind and helpful child doing a good deed, but why didn't he linger for a thank you or for some reward afterwards? How on Earth did he disappear so quickly?

From that moment on, stories concerning babies and children held a growing fascination for me. I was already collecting angel stories from people from all corners of the world, but it soon became clear that stories sent in by children or about children were truly special because children live in a world where angels are real. 'Grown-up' doubt, fear and scepticism simply aren't there. Unfortunately, this innate ability to 'see' spiritually declines with age, but as this book will make abundantly clear, it doesn't have to fade away and we can all rediscover, nurture and cherish the child within.

## Young at Heart

The term 'inner child' is a clichéd one but, like a number of clichés, it resonates with truth. Carl Jung called the inner child 'the Divine Child', Emmet Fox called it 'the Wonder Child', Charles Whitfield called it 'the Child Within' and some psychotherapists call it 'the true self'. But what is it?

The inner child is the child you once were, the child who desired to be nurtured, cared for and loved. This child still resides within you, however old you are. It is the part of you that is sensitive, creative, emotional, spontaneous, playful, intuitive, passionate and enthusiastic, but it is also the part of you most in need of comfort, guidance, love and reassurance. Many of us lose touch with our inner child as we leave childhood behind, but it remains with us all our lives. We are all children at heart, innocently searching for meaning in life, and it is through our inner child that our guardian angels reveal themselves to us.

According to the Swedish mystic Emanuel Swedenborg there is no need to look outside ourselves to encounter angels, because angels are within us, waiting to be discovered. This book aims to bring together inner child and inner angel by showing that it is through our inner child that angels speak to us. In this way, with love, trust and the open mind and heart of a child, anyone, whether they are eight or 80 years old, can see, hear or sense the nearness of their guardian angel.

Therefore, in the pages that follow not only will you find miraculous stories about babies and children, but you'll also find miraculous stories about adults of all ages and at all stages in life. The thread linking all the stories in this book is that the people who submitted them all have the ability to see the world through the eyes of a child, whether they are young in years or not. Seeing the world in this way doesn't mean being childlike in the sense of being naïve or ignorant of the ways of the world, but it does mean having an open mind and the ability to feel things deeply and express them spontaneously, and it is this openness and emotional spontaneity that draws angels.

## True Stories

Another thread linking all the stories in this book is that they are all real-life stories based on fact, not fantasy. The first chapter outlines some of my own experiences, both in childhood and later in life. You'll see that even though I was born into a family of psychics and Spiritualists, and am in no doubt today that angels are real because I have encountered them both in my work and in my personal life, when I was a child I didn't see, hear or sense them. In fact it took quite a while for me to trust in angels and there have been many doubts and fears along the way.

I feel it is important for you to understand some of what I have experienced over the years and how this has brought me to where I am today. Although amazing things have happened to me, and I hope they will continue to happen as nothing gives me more joy and happiness, I'm not a medium, a psychic, an angel lady or a guru. I'm a very ordinary 44-year-old mum with two children – my son is eleven and my daughter is nine – and although some of the things I have experienced have been a direct result of my work as a paranormal writer, other things have simply happened. This has led me to believe that we are all born with the ability to see, hear and sense angels, and although many of us lose our sensitivity over the years, there are ways for us to reawaken and reclaim it. I guess what I am trying to say here is that by sharing some of my psychic journey with you, I hope you will see that anyone, however sceptical and whatever their age, background, doubts and fears, can have the profound connection with angels that is their birthright.

The rest of the book is a collection of true stories sent to me by people whose lives have been touched by angels in some way. These people come from all walks of life. Some, but by no means all, had a deep faith in angels before their angelic encounter, or were devoted to a particular religion (angelic spirits of goodness appear in most of the world's religions), but others did not describe themselves as religious in any way. Like so many people today they believed in something, but were not quite sure what. And there were those who believed in nothing at all.

The first few chapters focus exclusively on stories concerning babies, born and unborn, and very young children. Then the following chapters move on to stories about teenagers and adults encountering healing angels, or angels that intervened during times of crisis or danger, or angels that spoke to them through animals, dreams, signs or spectacular coincidences. Some of these stories were sent to me in response to my previous angel books, but others have been collected over the 25 years I have been researching and writing features, books and encyclopaedias about spirits, ghosts, angels, dreams and the psychic world. Everyone who contributed to this book, either by submitting a story or by allowing me to interview them, has touched me deeply with their truth and integrity. I am extremely grateful to everyone and if you can't find your story here I do apologize, it is simply because space would not allow. I do feel incredibly privileged to be given permission to share these experiences with a wider audience.

## The Power of Conviction

I've lost count of the number of times people have told me that there is always a perfectly rational explanation for encounters with the world of spirit. One of the most popular of these so-called explanations is that angels live only in a person's imagination. At first I expended a lot of energy trying to prove that angels were real. I would stress that angelic encounters had been recorded and illustrated in almost every culture for thousands of years. I would point to the vast number of angel stories I had gathered from around the world – after all, in a court of law a witness statement is taken as evidence. I would try everything I could think of, but it soon became clear that I was wasting my energy. At the end of the day angels are spiritual beings and their existence cannot be proved in a rational way to those who have closed their hearts and minds to their existence. Basically it all comes down to belief, and to those who believe, either because they have an affinity with the message of love angels bring or because their lives have been touched by angels in some way, no proof is needed. No explanation will ever have the power of their conviction.

Some of the stories you will read in this book are profound. Others will make you smile and others may make you shed a tear. Some will send a chill down your spine, others will amaze and astound you and even stretch your belief, but let me again reassure you that to the best of my knowledge every one is true. Although in some cases grammatical and editorial changes have been made, and names, dates and other personal details have been changed to protect the identity of those who wished it, all of these stories are the real deal. They demonstrate the myriad different ways that angelic encounters can transform people's lives and they all bring simple messages of hope, comfort and love and the reassurance that loved ones who have passed on are never far away.

Whether you have had an angelic experience yourself or not, I hope that reading these incredible stories about people whose lives have been transformed by angels, as mine has been and continues to be, will remind you that we are all spiritual beings. We are all born with intuition and psychic potential. I hope these stories will encourage you to listen more to your intuition and to laugh, love, open your heart and live your life to the full like a child again. I hope they will make you laugh, or cry, because every time a person is moved in some way by reading an angel story, angels fly closer to Earth, bringing with them their pure unselfish joy, love and laughter.

So, if you feel ready, prepare to be amazed and inspired by the stories in this book. As with my previous two angel books, working on it has renewed my connection to the realm of spirit and opened my eyes to new possibilities. It is my sincere wish that it will do the same for you by showing you that ordinary people like you and me can open their doors and their minds and their hearts to let in laughter, love and angels, and can see this world and the next through the bright eyes of a child.

# Angel Babies

# Chapter 1

# Growing Up Again

'When we are willing to live as adults in childlike
spiritual surrender, we are nurtured and
cared for so sweetly.'
**Karen Goldman**

I'd love to be able to say at this point that I saw angels
when I was a child, but sadly that simply wasn't the case.
Sure, I was born into a family of psychics and Spiritualists and always believed angels were close by, because
that is what I was taught to believe at an early age, but I
wasn't one of those children who levitated in my cot,
had nightly chats with angels or saw dead people in the
playground. I didn't even have an imaginary friend! I
was incredibly shy as a child and perhaps overly serious.
I didn't trust my imagination or intuition at all. Creative
writing lessons in class were pure torture. Obsessed with
lists and chores and 'to dos', I never allowed myself
much time to play or dream. It was only much later in

life that I learned the importance of balancing doing with dreaming.

One of my first memories – I must have been three or four – is taking everything out of the food cupboard and putting it back in colour-coordinated order, much to my mother's dismay when she found out later. Perhaps I unconsciously chose the role of the organizer and the practical, level-headed one in our family as some kind of counterbalance because I grew up in a rather alternative family where talk of angels was commonplace and nothing was ever planned or seemed certain. We were constantly on the move, never staying in one place long enough to put down firm roots. My dad was disabled and we lived on Mum's meagre earnings as a psychic counsellor and there were often days when we really didn't know whether we'd be able to afford food, let alone pay the bills. My mum was never worried, as she always believed that angels would provide – and they did, as somehow we always had a roof over our heads and food to eat – but as a child I worried endlessly about the haphazard, unpractical nature of our lifestyle.

## Falling Down

Despite being 'the practical and sensible one', I desperately wanted to be psychic and to see and sense things like my mother and brother, so I read books, attended meetings and meditated for hours. Nothing worked. It was like bashing my head against a brick wall. Although I was smart, developing psychic gifts was one challenge that hard work and discipline simply couldn't help me with. Inside I felt disappointed with myself. School was hard for me, as fitting in with the crowd didn't come naturally. Gradually I lost confidence in myself and self-doubt took over. Then around the age of 12 my world crumbled and my childhood disappeared forever. I developed an eating disorder.

Looking over my diaries from the time, I'm still astonished by how distorted my thinking was back then. The world around me was not as perfect as I wanted it to be and controlling food became my way of coping. For the next four or five years I was on a painful journey. Although my weight never fell so low that I was admitted to a psychiatric hospital, I experienced life as a joyless battleground. Every day was a battle – to get out of bed, to get dressed, to function. At times my head was filled with thoughts of death, as it seemed to offer some kind of freedom. Every move I made was controlled by a relentless voice in my head. Regulating my food intake and my weight became my sole focus and nothing else seemed to matter. And in the process I lost everything. Any friends I did have disappeared, unable to understand or handle what was going on in my head. I also missed a lot of school as the once together and organized child disappeared into oblivion.

Thinking now about those dark and bleak days, I can see that even though I felt lost and alone and abandoned, angels were always there guiding me. I simply didn't have the eyes to see them or the ears to hear them or the heart to receive them. They manifested their loving presence first and foremost through my family. I took it all for granted at the time, but I don't know where I'd have been without my mother, who quietly and anxiously supported me every step of the way, even if those steps were sometimes backward ones.

Angels also manifested their loving presence at the moment when I needed them the most, though I didn't realize it at the time. Only now, as I reflect back on a significant turning-point in my young life, can I see the hand of my guardian angel at work.

## Seeing the Light

One summer morning when I was 15 I woke up with a blistering headache. I had not allowed myself to eat and drink anything but apples and black coffee for five days.

4

The destructive and overwhelming voice of anorexia switched on the moment I opened my eyes, as it had done relentlessly for the past three years. Anorexia would tell me to do something and I would have to do it. It didn't matter what it was that I had to do; to me, anorexia was going to provide the solution to everything – or so I thought. This morning it told me to keep going with my apple and black coffee regime and to increase my exercise programme to four hours a day.

Wearily, I swung my legs over the side of my bed and felt for my hip bones, reassured that they felt sharp and defined. I looked up and noticed that I had forgotten to close the curtains the evening before and that the window was open. This was rather strange, because I had never forgotten to close the curtains before and I suffered from hay fever, so the windows in my bedroom were never left open in the summer. I wondered if my mum had opened the window, but then I remembered that she was staying overnight with friends. I'd been invited, too, but hadn't wanted to go. Mum had only agreed to go if I promised to call her regularly and eat a banana as well as an apple. I had called, but I hadn't eaten the banana and had no intention of doing so.

I moved towards the window, squinting as the sunlight hurt my eyes, and tried to draw the curtains, but I simply couldn't lift my arms. They felt too heavy.

I tried once again to draw the curtains, but it felt as if something was gently but firmly clamping my arms to my sides. So then I tried to slump back into bed, but my feet were rooted to the spot. I couldn't move an inch.

I don't know how long I stood there soaking up the morning sunshine, but it must have been at least half an hour. At first I struggled, but then I stopped fighting and simply stood there, allowing the sunshine to wrap itself around me. As I felt the warmth of the sun on my face, a sudden clarity came to me. I realized in that instant that if I continued down the road I was headed on, anorexia would eventually kill me. It was then that I promised myself I would never let it get to this point again.

From that day onwards my recovery was gradual but steady. I had made the decision to live. It took a while, but eventually mealtimes were no longer a battleground. My mum told me that an angel had drawn my curtains back, opened my window and wrapped its arms around me that morning, but although the thought comforted me I still couldn't quite believe it. My practical, logical side told me that I had simply forgotten to draw the curtains the night before and that food deprivation had made me too weak to lift my arms. My fearful, anxious self told me that I wasn't special or psychic enough for angels to bother with me. But even though self-doubt still plagued me, somehow my common sense and my zest for life had returned, and they grew stronger as time went by. There wasn't room for anorexia in my head anymore. I started to take better care of myself and gave myself permission to have a life again.

There was a lot of work to do in terms of building my self-awareness and self-esteem, but my psychic journey began that day I stood by the window in the sunshine. I still didn't think I would ever see, hear or sense angels, but my mum, who had seen and spoken to angels all her life, used to tell me that when I was ready to open my heart and my life to them they would appear. I doubted her then, but years later I realized that she was right.

However, it took a good 20 years before I was finally ready to let angels into my life. In the meantime I was simply too anxious, fearful and lacking in self-trust. The harder I tried to sense angels, the further away they seemed to be and the more abandoned I felt. What I did not realize was that all along angels were guiding my life through my dreams, my intuition and the 'coincidences' that happened to me, but I was too full of questions, insecurity and fear to acknowledge those experiences for what they really were – the voice of my guardian angel.

The full story of my spiritual awakening and how the voice of an angel saved me from certain death can be found in my previous books; for now, all that it is neces- sary to know is that as a child and young adult my inner eyes were tightly closed. It was only when I learned to relax and get a handle on my fear and self-doubt – or, to put it another way, to see the world again through the eyes of a trusting child – that they began to open. And then it was as if a psychic doorway had also opened and all the angelic sensations and incredible experiences I had longed for came flooding in. Then I knew what I had always known but had forgotten along the way. With a newfound lightness of spirit, I reclaimed my inner angel and the innate spirituality I had lost faith in.

The more I worked with and trusted my angels, the more they began to work their magic in my life. Opportunities came my way both in my personal and professional life and barriers broke down. It wasn't long before I was presented with one of the greatest gifts and responsibilities of my life when I was asked to gather inspiring true-life angel stories and string them together in a book. Until then I'd distinguished myself as a writer with bestselling encyclopaedias about dreams and the psychic world, but the new book, *An Angel Called My Name*, entered *The Sunday Times* top 10 bestsellers list within a week or so of release. My mailbag swelled with letters from readers keen to share their experiences. It became abundantly clear to me then that my angels had been waiting for this moment and my life had been building towards it.

I realized that my task was to collect angel stories and bring them to a wider audience, because every angel story is a miracle, a living testimony to heaven on Earth.

Each story demonstrates the very real presence of angels in our lives. Each can help people see that there is goodness in and beyond this world and that this goodness is more than a match for the pain, suffering and injustice we see all around us.

Although we have advanced technologically, the same cannot be said for our spirituality. Our inhumanity to each other has not been eliminated. We need a spiritual lift – a big one – to help us feel safe again. We need the restoration of our faith and trust – in one another as human beings, in love and in our ability to make humane and positive choices for ourselves and for others. In short, we need to hear about angels around and within us and the miracle of love and goodness they bring to the world.

## An Angel Child

I've fast-forwarded a little here in my excitement, so let's go back a decade or so now to one of my very first encounters with an angel child.

I'd made friends with a neighbour who had recently moved into a house two doors away from me. She was roughly the same age as me – in her early to mid-thirties – and she had a four-year-old daughter and was expecting her second child. I guess we bonded because at the time I was expecting a child too.

I'd known her for about a month when she asked me if I'd mind looking after her daughter while she treated herself to a haircut. Normally I'd have politely declined, as I wasn't very good with kids, but this time I welcomed the opportunity to spend some time with a young child. You see, even though I did want to be a mother, I'd never been very maternal. In fact I'd never even held a baby or played with a young child. I felt uncomfortable around children. I didn't think they liked me. If truth be told, I was a little apprehensive about becoming a mother and wondered if I was up to the task. I figured that it was high time I gave myself a trial run, so to speak.

When I arrived at my friend's house, she greeted me at the door. I'd seen Sophie, her daughter, a few times before, but we had not been formally introduced. She was like a little doll and said, 'Pleased to meet you,' with an adorable lisp. Then she laughed and laughed before saying, 'Abir says hello.' I looked at my friend and she shrugged her shoulders and explained that Sophie was 'at that imaginary friend stage' and I should just ignore her. But I was working as a magazine journalist gathering stories for a series of articles about the paranormal, and I was immediately fascinated. I had no idea where this fascination would take me.

As soon as my friend had hugged Sophie, told her to be a good girl and left for her appointment, I asked her to tell me more about Abir. She was happy to oblige and told me that Abir was an angel who came to her whenever she wanted to see her. Chills ran through my body and I grabbed a piece of paper and a pen from my bag. I knew this was important and that I needed to write down exactly what she said. I asked her to tell me about Abir and this is roughly the gist of it:

Abir is my angel and she comes to me. She's in this room now. Look just behind you. I always know when she is going to appear because whenever she is near she makes things smell fresh and lovely. She's very beautiful and always smiling. She thinks you should smile more.

Sophie then drew a picture of Abir with huge blue wings and a purple light surrounding her and said I could keep it as a present because it would remind me to smile when my baby was born.

There was so much more I wanted to ask her, but just as I was about to, her mother came back home looking crestfallen. There had been confusion at the hairdresser's and her appointment had been double booked. Being the kind person she was, she had decided to stand down for the other person and book an appointment another day. I told her that I'd be more than happy to sit with Sophie then. I showed her the picture she had drawn of Abir and she said I was welcome to keep it as she had quite literally hundreds. She opened a drawer and took out a dozen or so of Sophie's angel drawings to show me, and all of them had the same smiling face and wings. Then she told me something which made me feel sad and I wasn't sure why: she had a plan to knock 'all this nonsense' out of Sophie's head.

As the day wore on I could not keep away from the picture Sophie had drawn of Abir. Even though her story sounded incredible, I believed it was possible she could be in contact with an angel because she was obviously an intelligent child. I did some research on the name Abir and was amazed to discover that not only was it an extremely rare name that Sophie was unlikely to have heard of but that its meaning was 'fragrance'. Sophie had told me that things smelled fresh and beautiful whenever Abir appeared.

A few days later I looked after Sophie again when her mother went for her hair appointment. This time I sat with her at my own house. I was keen to talk about Abir, but Sophie was in the mood for playing, not talking, and had brought a sack of toys with her. I didn't want to push things, so after I settled her down in the front room I started to do some light cleaning and tidying up behind her. I was just about to throw away a bunch of shrivelled roses that had been standing in a vase for way too long when Sophie ran towards me and begged me not to because Abir would look after them. I felt it was easier to comply with her than go into a long explanation, so I left them where they were and forgot about them.

The next morning I couldn't believe my nose when I came down the stairs and was hit by the strongest rose aroma I had ever smelled. I went into my front room and couldn't believe my eyes: my roses looked resplendent. There were even beautiful pink buds where dead stalks had been the day before.

I couldn't wait to tell Sophie's mum about the roses, but when I did she told me that she knew I meant well but she didn't want to indulge Sophie's 'nonsense talk'. Respecting her wishes as a parent, I promised never to mention angels again when I met Sophie. I stuck to my promise and Sophie didn't seem unduly distressed, especially once her mother had bought her a puppy to play with. Later I discovered that she'd been promised the dog if she never mentioned Abir again. I felt sad but whenever I saw Sophie with her new pet I liked to think that her guardian angel was still with her, just in animal form.

## In my Dreams

A few weeks after my chat with Sophie, anxiety about becoming a mother began to get the better of me. I was an organized, tidy person and one thing I did know about babies was that they were untidy, chaotic, unpredictable and demanding. I was fine during the day when I was busy with my writing, but when I was relaxing in the evenings I worried about not being able to cope. I worried about labour and delivery. I worried about my child having an abnormality or dying during the pregnancy or labour. I worried about dying myself. I worried about whether I would bond properly with the baby, given that I didn't feel that comfortable around children. I worried that I would be a terrible parent. I worried about money. I worried about combining work with motherhood. I worried about what having a baby would do to my body and to my marriage. I think you get the picture. I was a worry wort and it was starting to make me ill.

One night after I'd been reading some pregnancy magazines full of advice and tips, I felt overwhelmed. A wave of panic took over. Voices in my head told me that I wasn't going to be able to handle this. My husband was away on business, so I had no one to cling to for reassurance. I lay down in bed, shaking and sweating, and pulled the covers over myself. I was finding it hard to breathe and my heart was beating so loudly it seemed as if it was going to burst out of my chest. It felt as though the whole world was swirling around me. My mouth had never felt so dry. I was absolutely convinced that I was either dying or going mad. Then I felt an overwhelming tiredness.

I must have fallen into a deep and heavy sleep, because when I woke up the next morning I felt calm and centred. I sat up, rubbing my eyes, and then looked down at my bump and gave it a gentle rub. As I did so, memories of a vivid dream flooded back into my mind.

In my dream I had been walking alone in the most beautiful countryside. It resembled the Lake District, a place dear to my heart. I decided to climb a mountain so I could get a splendid view from the top. The climb started easily enough, but soon I ran into difficulties. I hadn't been pregnant at the start of the dream, but I was now. I was hugely pregnant and struggling to put one foot in front of the other. Turning back wasn't an option, as when I looked behind me the path had disappeared. The only way was up.

Exhausted, I sat down. Then I became aware of a little boy tugging at my arms and telling me to get up. He was olive skinned and about five years old and had dark eyes like chocolate buttons. I told him I couldn't climb anymore but he just laughed and told me that I could. His belief in me was infectious and I found myself following him up the hill. He was right – it didn't seem so hard to climb then and before long I was at the top of the mountain. The view was spectacular. I turned around to look for the boy, but he had gone. I called out for him, worried that he might not have made it. I didn't see him again but heard his voice saying, 'You won't get it right all the time and that's fine by me.'

I must have woken up then because I couldn't remember any more of the dream, but the words 'You won't get it right all the time' really struck a chord. In a flash of insight – an 'aha moment', as it is sometimes called – I understood that becoming a parent was something I would need to learn as I went along. I wouldn't get it right all the time and shouldn't even try, because no one does. In any case, there was no right or wrong way to do things, just the way that suited me and my family. And if I did make mistakes I would learn from them, just as I would from the things that went right.

I'm not saying that after this dream the worrying stopped completely – it didn't – but I didn't have another panic attack and for the first time since I had found out I was pregnant I knew in my heart that things would work out fine for me and my family. And they did.

I've never forgotten that dream and I never will, because the moment my son was born with his olive skin and chocolate eyes I knew beyond doubt he was the little boy in my dream. It touches me beyond belief to know that he reached out to me in my hour of need even before he was born.

## 'Before I Was Born ...'

From the moment my daughter was born, two years later, I got the feeling that she wasn't new to all this. You've probably heard the term 'old soul' before and it is certainly true that many children appear wise beyond their years. Some, especially those below the age of five, also seem to have an awareness of a time before they were born. My daughter was one of them.

Like me, my daughter was not prone to fantasy or make-believe as a child. She was practical, pragmatic and had a firm sense of right or wrong, always reporting in detail the truth or facts of a situation. That's why I couldn't have been more shocked when she was about four and a half and started to tell me about her life as an angel before she was born. She used to tell me that she watched over me and picked me to be her mummy and my partner to be her daddy and her brother to be her brother. By then I'd learned not to discourage or feel confused and scared by this kind of talk, as Sophie's mother had been. In fact I actively encouraged it. I told my daughter how lucky she was to have had such a special time and how glad I was that she had chosen me for her mother.

My daughter will be ten next year and no longer talks about her life before she was born. It all slipped away when she was about seven. At about the age of six, however, she shared a new revelation with me when she told that she had a guardian angel now and she often saw her standing in the garden with huge strong wings wrapped around the house. I trust that even though she doesn't mention her anymore she's still there and that there are yet more angels surrounding my daughter and my son, keeping them safe and lighting their way.

## A Special Connection

Because of my experience with Sophie and with my own children I had to know if other children interacted with angels in the same way. I remembered that my brother used to chatter to me about his angels when we were growing up together but, being his sister, I never paid much attention to anything he said! Now I asked for his help in my research, though, as he had become a secondary school drama teacher. I myself had been a secondary school English teacher for several years, so between us and two primary school teachers we knew, we conducted a brief informal, anonymous and voluntary survey of children from schools in our areas. What we discovered was breathtaking.

I simply asked children between the ages of 4 and 18 to tell me about angels in as few or as many words as they felt comfortable with. I also asked them to draw pictures of what angels looked like to them, if they wanted to. As expected, children over the age of 12 were less forthcoming as far as drawing pictures was concerned, but when it came to submitting stories, the teenagers were as willing to contribute as the younger children. This surprised me a great deal, as I had expected the majority of my submissions to come from the under tens, but it became clear to me that a particularly close bond exists between angels and teenagers as well as between angels and young children. In taking the time to explore these stories, a cross-section of which you will read later in this book, I discovered that angels appear to young people in some vivid and non-traditional ways. They aren't always white winged and wearing halos; they are as rich and varied as the children who experience them.

I wanted to talk to children with different lives outside my area, so I continued to gather stories from children across the country from a wide variety of backgrounds. All of them shared their stories with candour and conviction, and my desire to share their words and images with a wider audience grew stronger and stronger. In fact, finding out about children's encounters with angels was a catalyst for me, because children are still connected to a world so many of us have forgotten. I truly hope that reading their stories in this book will encourage parents, carers, teachers and anyone who comes into contact with children to honour and nurture their spirituality.

But it is not just validating children's spirituality that has become my passion. I'm just as passionate about validating spirituality in adults, but what working with children has shown me is that they can teach us so much more about spiritual growth than we can ever teach them. Perhaps this is all part of an angelic plan. Sometimes the best lessons are taught by those who don't think they have all the answers, but do know how to live simply and to the full.

## Growing Up Again and Again

Much of my childhood and early adult life was lost in worry and anxiety. Having children of my own has helped me rediscover and nurture the child inside me, the part of me through which angels speak, but something I also learned while gathering and researching angel stories is that it is not necessary to have children to grow spiritually. All of us, whether we are parents or not, can reclaim the unquestioning openness of a child that helps them see what adults often can't. All of us can grow up time and time again by reconnecting to the little child that still lives in us.

So what can children, whether inner or outer, teach us? First and foremost is simply to be. Children are masters at just being, living in the now, something we all tend to find harder and harder as we get older and responsibilities pile up. They are also willing to let the past go and let grudges go with it. This is a happy way to live.

In addition, children have the divine ability to freely give their love – no matter what. For me, before I had my children, the idea of unconditional love was just that – an idea. But by giving them unconditional love and receiving it in return I finally felt worthy of being loved and of loving *myself* unconditionally. I also learned how to forgive myself for the mistakes I'd made. My children taught me that. They have also shown me the rich rewards of opening my mind and filling it with new things, thoughts and ideas every day, but above all they have reminded me to give life everything I have. No matter whether I succeed or fail at a particular task or project, it is all a learning experience. But if I put a lot of time and effort into something I love, I will always find success because I will know, deep down in my soul, that I gave it everything I could.

All these qualities – the ability simply to be, to love unconditionally, to have an open mind and to live every day with passion, enthusiasm and a spirit of adventure – nurture and sustain that special bond between angels and children. And if as adults we can rediscover these qualities within ourselves, we too can stay young in spirit and reclaim our special bond with heaven, a bond that is our birthright.

## Tread Lightly

Children seem to accept angelic encounters with far more equanimity than adults, perhaps because they have not yet experienced a clear division between the two worlds and are therefore, for a little while, a part of each. Sadly, as they grow older and acquire greater knowledge, many lose their innate spirituality and become unwilling to take things at face value anymore. The acquisition of knowledge as we age is not necessarily a negative thing, but it can work against nurturing the childlike qualities of open-mindedness, enthusiasm, trust and emotional spontaneity that draw angels nearer to us. It is, however, possible to grow older in years without losing touch with the child in your heart.

One of the greatest spiritual leaders in the world is the Dalai Lama. A journalist friend of mine who spent a week with him told me that his booming laughter echoed from behind closed doors and down corridors. It was a genuine, bewitching, spontaneous laugh. My friend had expected this great man to be serious and intense, but he was exactly the opposite. There was a twinkle, a child in his eyes.

Years ago, when I regularly attended courses, lectures and conferences, all too often the heaviness and serious-ness of everyone involved weighed me down both spiri-tually and physically. I used to feel the same when I attended religious services, especially when reciting prayers in school assemblies. Everyone would bow their heads and mumble the words, often without feeling or thought, even when the words were beautiful. On one yoga retreat I attended I don't think I heard anyone laugh for the whole ten days. It felt somehow wrong to me and made me start to think that perhaps I too was guilty of approaching the subject of spiritual development with far too heavy a hand. My research on children has shown me that the angels are attracted to children because of their openness but also because of their laughter, enthusiasm and energy. Perhaps all those years I had been too intense and serious, too 'grown up' if you like in my approach. I didn't appreciate that when we laugh and experience joy we are closer than ever to our angels.

Perhaps because we're dependent on gravity to keep us grounded on Earth we tend to become weighed down with the serious and heavy stuff, sometimes to the point of taking ourselves too seriously and becoming self-important. Angels are charged with important work – the spiritual tasks of responsibility, courage, dedication, truth, justice, commitment, patience and education – but they carry them out lightly, going about them with joy, celebration, spontaneity, wonder, freedom, openness and love. It's often said that angels can fly because they take themselves lightly. This doesn't mean they don't have gravitas, just that they complete serious tasks with a lightness of spirit that comes from complete trust in the power of love.

Staying light in spirit and young at heart is not always easy, especially when life weighs you down with obstacles, pain and heartache, but angels have also taught me that life is not easy and it wasn't meant to be. If there were no problems, no setbacks and no heartaches, how would we learn and grow spiritually? But if we can face the challenges life throws at us with the open trusting heart of a child, angels will stand by us even in the darkest hours of our lives and give us the courage, optimism, energy and hope to pull through. The meaning of the word 'angel' is 'messenger', and the messages they bring are always ones of reassurance, love, comfort and the knowledge that we are never alone in this life or the next. For those who believe (and there are many of us who do), just the thought of their presence, the very idea of them, is somehow comforting and adds a sweetness and lightness to our lives.

## The Mark of an Angel is Love

I hope you will be as comforted and inspired and deeply touched as I have been by the stories I've included in this book. I hope they will encourage you to reclaim your inner child and grow up again with your guardian angel by your side, guiding you and watching over you.

If you don't know where to find your guardian angel, just remember the mark of an angel is love. Angels are everywhere and they are always trying to communicate with you. They manifest their presence in your life through every smile, every heart, every act of kindness, every good thought and unselfish desire and every warm spontaneous feeling. Wherever there is love, growth and optimism, angels will be there.

Maybe you've just been looking in the wrong places and have been too busy to see that your guardian angel has been there before your eyes and in your heart all the time.

# Chapter 2

# Angel Babies

'The world begins anew with every birth.'
**Sebastian Fawkes**

You may have heard about or read incredible rescue stories involving babies or very tiny children where angelic intervention seems the only possible explanation. Here are some sensational stories that caught the headlines in recent years.

## Saved by a Nappy

In August 2008 a baby fell 30 feet from his third-floor apartment building in the Brazilian city of Recife but was saved by a disposable nappy. Somehow the nappy snagged on a security spike embedded in the concrete wall around the building and broke his fall.

According to a police officer interviewed at the time, the boy dangled from the spike for a moment, then the nappy slowly opened and the baby fell to the ground at a much slower speed. 'It was a miracle,' said the officer. 'He could also have been killed by one of the spikes.'

The child was treated for minor fractures at the Hospital Memorial São José. His father believed that it was God who had saved his son and many commented that it must have been his guardian angel.

Some of you may also recall the well-reported story of 13-month-old Liam Evans during the summer of 1998. It left everyone amazed and once again the newspaper headlines talked of miracles and guardian angels.

## Staying Alive

For three days Liam survived on a mountainside, living off handfuls of soil, after a car driven by his grandfather plunged off the road. Liam landed uninjured in the soft undergrowth, but sadly his grandfather died instantly.

After three days and nights on his own, Liam was found by a young boy. The newspapers reported that he had survived because the thick bracken he had fallen into had protected him from the sun by day and the cold by night and the soil had provided enough moisture to keep him alive.

Another baby-related incident that got a lot of press coverage a few years back in 2005 was an amazing story from Africa.

## Baby Angel

In a tale that could have been lifted from the pages of a children's storybook, five-month-old baby Angel was left alone in a Nairobi forest for two days and was found and cared for by a five-year-old dog foraging for food.

Witness Stephen Tova told the independent *Daily Nation* newspaper that he saw a dog carrying a baby wrapped in a black dirty cloth crossing the road. He was shocked at first and was trying to get a closer look when the dog ran through a fence and disappeared along a dirt road. The baby was later discovered by two children when they heard the sound of a baby crying near their wood and corrugated-iron shack. They alerted some adults and the baby was found lying next to the dog and her own pup.

At the time many people talked about guardian angels taking steps to ensure this baby lived, but the implications of this miracle reached far wider than the child involved because it drew a lot of attention to the desperate problem of abandoned babies in poverty-stricken areas of Kenya.

Then there are incredible stories of babies inexplicably surviving car crashes.

## A Miracle!

In 2006 a seven-month-old baby was thrown through the back window of a car and bounced nearly 250 yards in his car seat down the fast lane of a dual carriageway near Teignmouth, Devon. Cars travelling at high speeds avoided him and he emerged from the ordeal with only a small bump on his head. Later, his father said it was 'a miracle' his son had not been killed. 'Someone must have been looking down on us,' he added.

## Another Miracle Baby

In December 2008, newspapers in Sweden also talked of a 'miracle baby'. This child survived a horrific crash when a car somersaulted into a ditch alongside the E18 motorway near Stockholm on Christmas Day.

All these stories were picked up by the media, but similar ones have also been sent to me over the years. They include incredible stories of babies surviving car, plane and train crashes or runaway prams being returned to safety by unseen hands. The following three stories, the first sent to me all the way from Australia by John, the second e-mailed to me by Karen and the third sent in by Amelia, are fairly typical – if there is such a thing as typical – of miracle baby-rescue stories.

## Caught by an Angel

I was carrying my son Jake in his car seat across the road when I was hit by a car. I was hurled into the air and so was Jake. He must have been thrown about ten feet or so. Incredibly, neither of us was seriously hurt. It's a miracle we are alive and have no broken bones. All I can remember is hearing a loud noise and then being thrown. When I got up, my first thought was for Jake. Everyone says thank goodness he was well strapped into his car seat, but I say thank goodness our guardian angels were close by.

Like John, Karen is convinced that her baby has a guardian angel.

## The Angel on the Escalator

This is one of the strangest things, if not *the* strangest thing that has ever happened to me, and my best friend's sister said something similar happened to her as well, so there must be angels working on escalators. It happened when my daughter was five months old. I was out shopping with my sister, as I figured I needed a bit of a treat, but as any mum knows, shopping with a baby involves carrying a lot of stuff: nappies, pushchairs, wipes, bottles, a change of baby clothes and so on and on. The toughest task for me, though, was getting up and down the escalators with the pushchair. Normally I'd have taken the lift, but it was very crowded that day so I decided to take a risk and use the escalator instead.

My sister got onto the escalator and then I rolled my pushchair onto it with my daughter strapped in. A teenage boy with his iPod playing got on behind me and although I was aware that he was two or three steps behind and wearing a white hood, my main focus was on keeping my pushchair upright.

When we got to the bottom my sister got off and I began to roll the pushchair off behind her, but I felt a little dizzy and lost my balance. I fell over and my body weight pushed the pushchair away from me at speed and hurled it over to one side. I ended up on all fours with a very painful pair of knees.

I got up and for a moment or two froze with fear. I could hear my heart beating but not my baby crying. I ran to my pushchair, which had skidded several feet from the bottom of the escalator, and it was empty. I turned around and standing at the bottom of the escalator was the boy in the white hoodie, holding my little girl in his arms. She was fine and smiling. Still shaking, I took her and covered her with kisses. I can't have looked away for more than a few moments, but when I looked up again to thank him and ask him how he had got her out of the pushchair so fast, he had gone.

I asked my sister, who by now had rushed to my side, if she knew where the boy had gone and she said she hadn't seen a boy. She said I had got my baby out of the pushchair, but I know that it hadn't been me but the boy. I ran ahead and looked for him, but there was no trace of him.

This remarkable story sent to me by Amelia also features a pushchair.

## Hit Really Hard

This happened to me last month and I had to write and tell you about it. I'm a psychologist and have never believed in angels or any of that stuff. I thought it was all wish fulfilment or imagination, but everything has turned upside down for me now and I'm willing to believe the impossible can happen.

I was staying with my husband's family in Austria and decided to take my young son for a walk in his pushchair. I walked for a while along a main road and then decided to cross over. There were no cars coming so I started to walk across. As I did so, though, I heard a car coming extremely fast from the right. I had no chance of getting away. With a presence of mind I didn't think I had, I pushed the pushchair away from me so that at least my son would be saved and then I ran after it. I must have pushed too hard, though, as the pushchair bounced off the curb and started to roll back into the road. At the same time I slipped and fell, banging my head. We were both going to die.

Then a woman ran out from the pavement and stepped in front of the car. The driver obviously saw her, because he tried to swerve but didn't quite make it and the woman was hit hard and thrown into the air. The driver then lost control and skidded into a brick wall, crushing the car and very probably himself. This all happened really quickly while I was still trying to get up.

As soon as I was up, my first instinct was to run to my baby and pull the pushchair out of the road. There was blood trickling down my face from where I had fallen and I must have been hysterical.

By then a police car had pulled up by the crash scene, followed by several others. Later I would learn that they had been chasing the driver of the car, as he was a dangerous car thief. They started to pull him out of the car and his body was limp and bloody. This made me think of the woman who had stepped out into the road. The force with which the car had hit her must have caused terrible injuries. I looked round, but I couldn't see her anywhere. I asked the policemen to look but they couldn't find her either. The only other person who had seen her was the driver of the car, but he died two days later in hospital, leaving me as the only witness.

People say the bang on my head must have caused hallucinations, but I know what I saw and I believe that woman was an angel. I wasn't imagining it, whatever people say, and I know she saved my life and the life of my son.

Miraculous baby-rescue stories may force even the most sceptical of people to at least consider the possibility that something or someone not of this world is watching over a child. But as sensational as stories like this are, they are also fairly rare. Far more common but less well known are stories where babies are not in life or death situations yet still have guardian angels watching over them.

## What Were They Looking At?

While I have been researching and writing this book, countless parents have told me they believe that babies have the ability to see angels or the spirits of departed loved ones. They believe this because they have seen a baby, either their own or someone else's, stare at a particular spot in a room, typically the ceiling, and appear captivated by it, occasionally smiling or cooing as if they are communicating with someone invisible. Sometimes the baby will even lift their arms towards the invisible presence as if wanting to be picked up. Adults can't see anything themselves and cannot explain it.

There is plenty of documented evidence to suggest that babies do often behave in this manner and over the years I've received hundreds of stories from parents who have witnessed their babies clearly seeing something special. In my opinion there are just too many stories out there, like this adorable one sent to me via e-mail by Whitney, to discount the fact that something special is going on.

## Looking Up

Last night at about 11 o'clock when I was feeding my twin baby boys I needed to burp them, so I put them down in their cot to get a blanket to put over my shoulders. The moment I put them both down, they started to squirm and fuss. I started to feel tense, because I couldn't find any blankets and I'd hardly had any sleep the last few weeks.

Then suddenly they both stopped fussing at the same time and there was complete silence. This was very odd, as they'd been suffering from colic for a week or so and either one or both would be squirming for attention at any given moment. I looked down and saw them both staring at the right-hand corner of the room. I looked where they were looking and there was nothing there apart from dust, and there was no way they could see that with their newborn eyes. Rays of moonlight were creeping in from the window, but they were not looking at any pockets of light.

What were they looking at that made them both settle down at exactly the same time? Even stranger was that I felt as if something was saying to me that they didn't need to be burped and they would sleep better now.

It's six in the morning now and I am up by myself and have been able to shower and wash and blow dry my hair after sleeping for a good six hours. I haven't been able to do this since the twins were born.

My daughter, who's five now, also had a habit of looking intently at a corner of the room when she was a newborn. It wasn't the same corner as the one the twins were looking at, as we were living in a different place then, but it was still a corner. So if babies do see angels, I think they like to hang out in corners.

Whitney's experience is fairly typical of the amazing stories about babies seeing angels that I've gathered over the years. I never tire of reading these stories, not just because it lifts my spirits each time I picture in my mind the wonder and delight new parents experience when they witness their babies behaving in this way, but also because they bring back memories of the many times late in the evening when I was feeding my own babies and they would suddenly pull away, even when they were ravenous, and focus on something invisible to me. Sometimes they would stare intently, but other times they would smile as if they were being entertained. How I longed to join in with them and see what they were seeing.

On other occasions my son would be in the middle of playing with his toys and stop to stare at nothing in particular. He would then start to babble and coo into thin air. At the time I did wonder if tricks of the light were a factor or if there was some other perfectly rational explanation, but ever since I've found out that this 'stop and stare at something invisible' phenomenon, as I like to call it, is far more common than I thought. I'm now convinced that babies have an innate ability to 'see' at a spiritual level. Here's Nadine's story:

## Taking an Angel Home

I had heard stories of babies seeing angels and spirits but had never really given them much thought. I can't say if I believed in them or not. I believe in them now and want to tell you about my eight-month-old cousin called Grace. Last week I was getting her ready to leave the house and she was sitting up on the bed and fussing a little. I noticed that she was staring at the cupboard door behind my back and giggling and cooing as if there was someone there. I was intrigued and sat down beside her. She didn't seem to notice me at all, as she was enchanted by the cupboard door. I tried to get her attention by bouncing a little on the bed, but she wasn't interested. Then, as if her eyes were following something leaving the room, she leant forward and looked at the door. Then she giggled and turned back to me.

After seeing that, I believe my little cousin has an angel watching over her. I don't live with her, but I look after her every Saturday. So from now on when I go to pick her up I'll know that as well as her nappies and bottles I'll be taking an angel home with me.

I can't bring myself to move on at this point and would just like to share a few more special baby angel stories with you, like this one from Ally.

## Angel Eyes

When my eldest daughter was about seven months old I remember something very weird – or should that be wonderful – happening. I was a young single mum then. My boyfriend had walked out as soon as I told him I was pregnant. He didn't want the responsibility of a child. I was determined to keep the baby, though, even though I was worried sick about how I was going to make things work on my own.

One day I was hugging my daughter and playing with her when for no reason at all I started crying. I looked down at this precious child and wondered how on Earth her father could have deserted her. I wiped away my tears, concerned that I might upset my daughter, but she had a huge amused smile on her face and was looking behind me. I turned around, but there was nothing there. I looked back at her and started to gently tickle her to get her attention. As I was looking into her eyes I could see my own reflection, but there also seemed to be the reflection of a tall figure standing there.

I turned around immediately, but couldn't see anything. Then, when I turned back to my daughter, it was as if my whole mindset had turned around. Instead of feeling that the world was a fearful place I felt that it was a wonderful, loving place and that my daughter would be taken care of.

Things got better for me after that day. I finally got a job and was offered flexible hours so that I could look after my daughter. Two years later I married my boss and we have been together 30 years now. I had two more children with him. My daughter is all grown up now with children of her own, but I like to think that the figure I saw in her eyes was her guardian angel and that she is still being looked after today.

Ally's vivid story has a certain similarity to Wanda's story below. Wanda's world also changed for the better after she looked into her baby's eyes.

## Baby Tim

My first child was born three years ago, a boy called Tim. When he was a tiny baby he used to sleep in the same room as my husband and me in a basket. I was absolutely terrified that he would stop breathing in the night. I'd heard so many horrible stories about how cot death could strike at any time and my son was so tiny that I didn't think he was very strong.

I was having trouble sleeping anyway because he needed to be held when he fell asleep, so I would hold him for a long time. When my husband wasn't working nights he would help out, but even when both of us were around Tim would still wake up two or three hours later wanting to feed. After a few months we moved on to bottled milk so we could both do the feeding, but even this was difficult. Life was a blur of tiredness.

To make matters worse, often I would panic, thinking that I couldn't hear my son breathing. So I would have to get up, go over to the basket, grab a torch and check to see that his little chest was rising and falling. Then I would tiptoe back to bed. If I couldn't fall asleep I'd be up again checking the breathing. My husband and I were both exhausted and he was getting mad at me because whenever he wanted to fall asleep he would be woken by the baby or by me getting out of bed, fumbling with the torch and checking on him.

I knew my fear was silly and irrational, but it became a compulsion. At one point when my husband was working I remember getting up every 20 minutes or so and then eventually falling asleep with the light on. That morning I woke up a good hour or two later than normal. My heart beating wildly, my first thought was to check on my son. I found him lying on his back with his eyes wide open staring at the ceiling and cooing. He looked perfectly content and I watched him for a while. Our ceiling is painted white and there are no patterns there or indeed anything interesting that I think could have caught his attention, but it really looked as though he was being entertained by someone or something.

I picked him up and sat down to feed him, but even though it was a good two hours later than his normal feed time he showed no signs of wanting to feed. Instead he just looked at me with his huge eyes and there was a hint of a smile on his face. We stared at each other like this for a good ten minutes and I know this sounds crazy but in those ten minutes it felt as though my little son was telling me that he was being looked after. Eventually he closed his eyes and I put him back in his cot.

After that I didn't stop worrying completely – I don't think any mum ever does, however old her children are – but I realized I was only making things worse by worrying so much. The compulsive checking stopped completely and I managed to get a bit more sleep, which, as any parent of a baby will know, is a miracle in itself.

Although neither Ally nor Wanda could actually see angels looking down on their children, complete with bright lights, feathered wings and a halo, both truly believe that guardian angels were watching over them and that the babies knew it.

Eliot is also convinced that his baby son is seeing something. Here's his story:

## Definitely Seeing Something

Every night after I bath my 19-month-old son Tyler I lay him down on the living-room sofa to put on his nappy and pyjamas. For the last five days while he has been lying there he has been staring up at the ceiling and saying, 'Babies'. When I ask him what he is looking at, he just smiles, points up at the ceiling and says, 'Babies' again. Then when I've finished changing him and he's ready for bed he waves his hand and says goodbye to the babies.

He's definitely seeing something and I think they are angel babies because he gives them such a huge smile and laughs as if they are doing something funny for him. It's a beautiful thing to watch and every night I can't wait to see if the angel babies are going to visit him again.

Pam thinks her son has seen angels too. Here's what she wrote in an e-mail she sent to me:

## Spellbound

My baby boy did this quite often – as many as 10 or 12 times a day. It started when he was about five weeks old and tailed off when he was about seven months old, although some days he was at it again. It was always the same. He would be looking at something, utterly entranced, and have a joyful smile on his face. Whatever he was seeing was invisible to me. He didn't always look at the same spot and it could happen at any time. I tried to see if there was anything that could be catching his eye, but I never could.

I've heard that babies can see angels because they don't have the disbelief and hang-ups that cloud the eyes of adults and I do like to think that he was looking at his own personal guardian angel.

My husband thinks I sound weird when I talk about things like this, but it's been wonderful to find out that other mums have had the same experience. I don't know why, but it's given me an enormous amount of comfort. I miscarried four times before my son was born and until he started seeing things I was terrified something might happen to him, but now I know he's being looked after and protected.

Often when I get letters or e-mails from parents about their babies or children, I find that, as with Pam, talk of angels and the world of spirit is new to them but also strangely familiar and comforting. At first many of them question and analyze and try to explain their infant's behaviour rationally, because, as was the case with Michelle, something happens which seems so strange.

## Sounds Strange?

This may sound strange to you, because it still sounds strange to me, but it really happened. I'd just put my daughter Ashley, who is nearly two, into her high chair and had left it pulled out from the table because I didn't want her to start grabbing her meal yet. I turned away to get her juice and some wet wipes and when I turned round she was pushed in and already eating. When I asked her who had pushed her in she said, 'Oma'. I nearly dropped the juice because I always used to call my grandmother Oma (I'm Dutch Indonesian and Oma is the word for grandma I used when I was growing up) and as far as I can remember I had never spoken of her to Ashley.

She died when I was about ten years old. I do remember her, though, and my mum always used to say to me that the first time I had solid food it was my grandmother who fed me.

Jessica also found her baby had a link with someone who had passed on:

## The Entertainer

My daughter is 14 months and as soon as she was old enough to babble she would talk to pictures of my father. I didn't think there was anything unusual about this, but then a month or so ago she said she had seen an angel. I asked her what it had been doing and she said juggling. Then I asked what it had looked like and she pointed to a picture of my father.

My eyes filled with tears of joy, because although my father died before I was born, my mother told me that he used to be a brilliant juggler. I haven't talked about him to my daughter yet and my mother certainly hasn't, as she lives abroad and the last time she saw my daughter was eight months ago, but I'm so happy my daughter is getting to know her grandfather and being entertained by his juggling.

It is very heart-warming that some babies not only see their guardian angels but get to play with them as well. Here's Reuben's story:

## 'Play with Me'

My son has just turned one and from the day he came home from hospital he has always been looking at little things around the room that we can't see. At the moment he is really into playing 'peek a boo'. Last night, when I peeked through the door of his room to check he was alright, I realized that he was actually playing boo with someone I couldn't see. I went into his room to play it with him, but he wouldn't play with me! I felt really put out at first, but then I had to smile.

Sam is also delighted that her toddler, Sally, has a playmate. Here's what she told me:

## Sally and Sammy

A couple of weeks ago when my husband was giving Sally a little massage on her back she jumped up and started to look around her as if she was looking for someone. This isn't unusual – in fact it happens so often that we have called the invisible person Sammy. I'm not sure who or what Sammy really is, but ever since Sally started playing with him/her/it, she's not been frightened of the dark anymore. She used to scream and scream at night and I got really worried about her, but now we have the most peaceful nights ever.

Many parents tell me that a beautiful calm descends over their babies when they see their guardian angel and this stops them stressing about the apparent strangeness of it all. In fact, the babies almost always appear more settled and happier afterwards, which suggests to me that it is a perfectly natural experience. Jane sent me this story which beautifully illustrates the point:

## 'Missing You'

When Lucy was born we had no idea how Simon, our five year old, would react to the baby and the change in the family dynamic, as he was a much longed-for and adored child who was used to being the centre of attention. When we brought her home we told him that he should not be near her unless one of us was present.

One day he disobeyed us and went into her room. We soon noticed he had gone and searched the house. As soon as we got upstairs we heard him talking in a quiet voice to Lucy. We tiptoed to the nursery door to watch him and listen to what he was saying. We heard: 'Can you tell me about the angels again, because they were always with me, but I don't see them anymore and I miss them.'

It seems we are all born with the ability to see angels but as we grow older we stop believing what we are seeing. Some of us do remember what we've seen, but some of us don't. It's a bit like dreaming. All of us dream but only some of us remember our dreams. Some people don't think they dream at all, but they do. They just can't remember.

Babies can see angels as soon as they open their eyes, but until they are about three they can't communicate well enough to let anyone know what they are seeing. And then they find out that their parents and teachers can't see what they see. This can be a shock and can lead to self-doubt. Then there is a process that narrows their psychic gifts even more – let's call it conditioning. This is when many children are told that an apple is red, an orange is orange, some things are real and some things, like angels and spirits, aren't. Children are incredibly receptive at this stage and keen to please their parents, so if they are told often enough that what they are seeing isn't real they will lose their ability to see, hear and sense angels.

Instead of worrying or feeling anxious, parents should try to cherish the fact that their infant sees angels close by and should allow them to strengthen that special connection with the world of the invisible. It is a perfectly natural thing for babies to see people who were with them before they were born, or spirits who are about to be born into this world, or angels who are watching over them. After all, every baby is a miracle fresh from heaven.

# Chapter 3

# Unborn Angels

'A baby is an angel whose wings decrease
as their legs increase.'
**Author unknown**

In this chapter you'll see that the special bond between babies and angels isn't just created when they are born. It already exists in pregnancy and may even be there long before a child is born, conceived or even thought of by their parents. And if for some reason – abortion, miscarriage, stillbirth or some other misfortune – a baby dies in the womb or soon after birth, angels continue to watch over and protect that child in spirit.

## Angel Pregnancies

Falling pregnant is one of the most amazing but also life-changing episodes in a woman's life, so it is hardly surprising to me that so many letters and e-mails have come in regarding encounters with angels during this time. Having a baby is also potentially a period of spiritual growth for both mother and father, and angels always draw closer when they sense that a person is going through a period of great spiritual change and is in need of their support, reassurance and guidance.

My mother always told me that about two months before I was born she saw an angel in her room. It had beautiful orange wings. Eventually it vanished into the bookcase – perhaps an early indication of my future career as a writer? My mother told me it was her guardian angel. We always used to laugh about the fact that it faded into the bookcase, but my mother said it was very real.

Many stories have been sent to me by women who believe they met their guardian angel during pregnancy. Sometimes the angel appears in traditional form but in other instances it appears in the form of the spirit of a lost loved one. Gail told me about this visitation during her pregnancy:

## 'I Wasn't on my Own'

Fifteen years ago I was pregnant with my daughter and was living alone in a flat in Leigh. I was very scared of the prospect of becoming a mum alone, but tried not to get stressed, as I had epilepsy and didn't want to have a seizure. Anyway, I started to dream about this man with a goatie beard. I recognized the man: it was my dad. It was the first time I had ever dreamed about him and I had barely known him, as my parents divorced when I was six months old and then my dad died when I was four years old.

Even stranger, one night I got up to use the bathroom and heard someone laughing in the living room. As I went in I saw my dad leaning on the TV just laughing. For about a week afterwards I could feel a presence in there, so I slept on the couch to see if he returned. He never did, but from that moment on I was so chilled out about having the baby. I asked my aunty, my dad's sister, if he had ever had a goatie, as I didn't have any photos of him with one, and she said he had had one a few years before he had married my mum. I told her what I had seen and she said she thought he was just letting me know that he was there and that I wasn't on my own.

Madison kindly took the time to write to me and tell me about a visit she had from an angel at the end of her pregnancy. But, as you'll see, was this her guardian angel or was it someone else?

## Somewhere in Time

I worked right up to the time my baby was due to be born. I own my own restaurant and I was scared that if I took my eye off the ball things would collapse. My due date came and went and my bag was packed for the hospital, but my baby didn't want to budge. The midwife told me that if it didn't come in the next week I would need to be induced.

Three days before my induction I stayed late at the restaurant to make sure everything was in place for a big booking the following day. I was filling out some forms when I thought I heard someone come into my office. I looked up and saw a young girl of about 14 or 15 in a white dress. The dress was solid but also translucent. The girl was stunning and it seemed as if bright light was shooting out of her hair. I noticed that she had blonde hair with a fringe unsuccessfully covering a red mark on her forehead that looked like a scar. She smiled and pointed at my bump, saying, 'Tomorrow's the day.'

Before I could ask her who she was or what she was talking about, she moved away and walked out of my office. Mesmerized, I followed her and saw her disappear into thin air. She seemed to glide, not walk.

The following day my daughter was born. The birth wasn't easy and forceps had to be used to pull her out. I was too exhausted to hold her right away, but later, when she was placed in my arms, I noticed that she looked a little battered and bruised and there was a deep gash on her forehead. Gently I placed my finger on it and the first words I whispered to her were, 'We've met before, haven't we?'

My daughter is going to be 18 next year and she still has the faintest mark on her forehead. People say I'm crazy, but I just know she visited me in spirit the night before she was born. We're incredibly close. From the moment I held her and saw the gash on her forehead, the strength of my love for her quite literally knocked me sideways. She looked so fragile and bruised, and although I had a nanny lined up, there was no way I was going to let anyone take care of her but me. I didn't stop working, but I found a way to take her to work with me and hired extra help when life got crazy busy. It wasn't easy juggling motherhood and work, but then nothing worth doing in life is.

Anja also met her daughter before she was born. She sent me this lovely story:

## Brown Eyes

I dreamed that I was standing with my boyfriend Liam in my apartment with a baby girl in my arms. Liam was right behind me looking at her over my right shoulder. We had made a bet on whose eyes she would have and were waiting for her to open her eyes to see who had won. Finally she opened them and I was moved in the deepest of ways, as her eyes were brown and looked exactly like mine.

I had this dream a year before we decided we wanted children and about a month after it I was told by my doctor that due to polycystic ovaries I might not be able to have children. My little girl already knew better, though. I feel sure she visited me in my dream to tell me that I could have a baby and that she would have the same brown eyes as mine.

Stories like these suggest that there may well be some kind of soul connection between a child and their parents before birth. Unborn children seem to have the ability to reach out across time and space.

And it's not just mothers who have seen their children before they were born – fathers have too. Simon wrote and told me the following story:

## 'Call Me'

I'm writing to you about a dream I had the night before my son was born. We thought we had the perfect name picked out for him: Brian. But then I had the dream and just had to rethink my choice.

In the dream I was waiting to pick my son up from a football match. I was shouting his name, but he didn't respond. Eventually I said, 'John!' and he turned around and said, 'Hi, Dad.' In the early days of my wife's pregnancy we had thought about calling a boy John for a while because it was my dad's middle name and by happy coincidence also my wife's dad's first name, but we eventually decided against it. My wife's boss at the time was called John as well and she didn't get along with him and really didn't want to be reminded of him in any way at home.

When the baby was born I told my wife about my dream and said how could we name him Brian after a dream like that? She still wasn't keen on the name John, but eventually agreed and our son was christened John Brian.

A year later to the day that my brilliant son was born, my wife's father was killed in a hit and run accident. We like to think he lives on in our son.

Another parent who wrote to me about a fascinating angelic experience during pregnancy was Nadine.

## A Story about Hope

I lost my beloved mother to cancer in December 1989 and before she died I promised her that if I had a daughter I would call her Hope and she would be our hope for the future.

In the middle of 1992 I found out I was pregnant, which was a surprise as I was just recovering from my second ectopic pregnancy and had been told I wouldn't be able to have any further children due to all the scarring.

Even after the doctors had confirmed that the baby was in the right place and was doing fine, I couldn't get rid of the fear of something going wrong. Then when I reached about seven months I started to have dreams in which I could see a baby crying in a cot but I wasn't allowed to go near it. I would wake up crying myself, feeling totally frustrated. I had this dream every night for over a month. One day I asked my mum in spirit to somehow let me know what was going on, as it was breaking my heart. That night I had the dream again, but this time I was allowed to go to the cot and look at the baby and I saw it was a dark-haired baby girl and my mother was standing next to the cot smiling.

When I woke up I felt at peace and I didn't have the dream again. But on 8 May 1993 I went into labour. The baby was born but didn't cry and I hadn't been able to see her arrive, so for a moment I panicked, but my husband said, 'Hope is here. Hope has arrived.' I didn't believe him, but the nurses confirmed it. Then she cried, and it was the same cry from my dreams and when they laid her in my arms it was the same baby and I felt a hand take the weight off my shoulders.

A week later, when I arrived home from hospital, there on my dressing table was an old photograph. It was a baby photograph of my mother and I realized that my daughter and my mother looked exactly the same.

Nadine believes that the miracles surrounding the birth of baby Hope had started several years earlier:

I had two ectopic pregnancies and the second one nearly cost me my life. At the maternity hospital the head of department wanted to remove my tubes and give me a hysterectomy and the young resident wanted to do an experimental procedure that had never been performed before. They stood arguing at the foot of my bed and the young resident asked me what I wanted to do. I told him to go ahead and do what he wanted, as someone had to be the first and it might as well be me, and that way I might just be able to have more children (the odds were 5,000 to 1).

After the operation I was very, very sick for a long time and no one really believed that it would work. But after that I was able to conceive naturally. I believe that this fantastic doctor was placed in my room by powers unseen, not only for me but also for other women so that they wouldn't have to go through the old heartbreaking way of dealing with an ectopic pregnancy. This doctor gave me and other women Hope.

Pregnancy isn't the only time in an expectant mother's life when angelic visitations are reported. They can occur at the moment of conception, as they did for Cassidy:

## The Answer to a Prayer

The story I'm about to tell you happened in 1971. My mother told it to me. My parents really wanted to have a child and they had been trying for nearly three years but nothing had happened. My mum eventually went to see the doctor to see if there was anything wrong. After a series of examinations he told her that there were abnormalities with her womb – it had not developed properly and was very small. He also told her that the chances of her getting pregnant, staying pregnant and having a healthy baby were very slim.

My mum always believed there was a guardian angel watching over her and she decided to pray to her and ask for a baby every night before she went to sleep and every morning when she woke up. I don't think my father really believed in angels, but he went along with the praying to keep Mum happy.

My mother was always a very deep sleeper, but one night she woke with a start. She looked up and standing next to her was a figure surrounded by white light so blinding that she had to shield her eyes. She looked at my dad, but he was snoring. She looked back at the figure and saw something move out from it like a hand and reach out towards her. She wasn't scared and just closed her eyes and when she did she felt a touch on her belly. When she opened her eyes again, the figure had gone. She fell into a deep sleep, only to be woken up by my dad a few hours later. He told her that he had had an incredible dream. In it he had been holding a baby in his arms and the baby had told him that there was a child on the way.

About two to three weeks later my mother found out that she was pregnant and in May 1972 she gave birth to my sister. The following May she gave birth to me. Until the day she died she would tell me that her guardian angel had answered her prayers for children. And I believed her.

## Divine Deliveries

Angels can also appear during delivery, as they did for Mia:

## Meeting Tom

My memories of angels date back to my childhood days. Then I played with a special angel I always called Tom. My mother used to laugh every time I asked for a sweet because I would always want two: one for Tom and one for myself.

Later, when I was pregnant myself, about four weeks before my baby was due I figured that as it had been a textbook pregnancy so far it was safe for me to have a night out with friends and maybe enjoy a drink or two. After my second drink I started to feel a bit dizzy, so I decided to call it a day and rang for a taxi to take me home. My friends helped me into it and we set off. The roads were very busy and I remember feeling quite sick as the car twisted and turned, and then my waters broke. I tried not to panic, as I'd read that it could be hours, days even, after the waters breaking before the baby arrived. To be on the safe side, though, I called my mum and asked the taxi to head to the hospital instead of my home. After that it's a bit of a blur. I must have passed out.

The next thing I remember is waking up in a hospital room. I was lying in a bed and there was a glowing light a foot above my head and a feeling of warmth in my chest. I didn't have a clue why I was there at first, but then I remembered my baby. A doctor came into the room with a look of disbelief on his face and walked to the side of the bed. He said my mother had gone to get a coffee and she would be thrilled to see me awake.

I apologized for going out to party. I knew I shouldn't have done it. The doctor smiled and said I had nothing to apologize for. He brushed the hair from my eyes and it was the softest, warmest touch I had ever felt in my life. I looked into his sparkling blue eyes and noticed he was wearing a hospital name tag with the name 'Tom Bright' on it.

Smiling, he turned and slowly walked out of the room. Then my mother came in and rushed to my side. I asked her what she knew about the doctor she had passed coming into my room, but she said there had been no doctor there. She sat down on the side of my bed and as she did so she picked up a long white feather which shimmered like none we had ever seen before. Later, when I asked the hospital staff about Dr Tom Bright, no one knew who he was, but in my heart I realized he was my guardian angel.

Over the next couple of hours I went on to deliver a fine healthy boy. I haven't seen my guardian angel since and I miss him, but in some ways I do see him every day, as I named my son Tom.

Teri had a very similar experience when she had her special delivery:

## 'Something Extraordinary Happened'

As my delivery date approached I was filled with anticipation and eager to move on with life as a mother, wife and student. I was nervous, of course, but confident that everything would work out despite the risk of potential complications. I've got a very small pelvis and scans indicated that my son's head was very large.

My contractions started a good three weeks before my due date. I was watching a movie at the time with my husband and he rushed me to hospital. My doctor was away at a medical conference and I felt my heart sink at the news. I knew my husband was nervous and would have much preferred to sit outside the delivery room, but with my mum delayed several hours by traffic it looked as though he was going to be the one by my side.

After what seemed like an eternity with no baby arriving, a doctor examined me and told me that my pelvis looked just too inflexible to deliver the baby. A Caesarean was offered, but the problem was the hospital needed to have blood on hand in case a transfusion was needed and there was none of my type available. The medical team tried to delay my labour with medication until the blood arrived and I was heavily sedated. I must have fallen into a deep sleep, because when I woke up it was very early in the morning and I could hear my husband snoring in the chair beside me.

I felt totally at peace, but then without warning a massive contraction gripped my body. I was in pain, but tried to push with all my strength. Nothing happened and I knew my baby was in trouble. I tried to call out to my husband to raise the alarm, but my mouth was so dry that no words came out. And then something extraordinary happened: a young doctor walked in and greeted me in a soft voice with an Eastern European accent. He told me that he was a medical student and that he was going to place his hands on my abdomen to stimulate an external contraction and help me push. That is what he did and at that moment my son was born.

At that point my husband woke up and, realizing what had happened, shouted for help. Within moments, a couple of nurses entered the room and started to examine the baby. My mouth was still too dry for me to speak properly, but I looked at the man who had delivered my baby and smiled my gratitude. I did notice, though, that no one spoke to him.

Later one of the nurses told me how relieved they were that I'd been able to deliver on my own but also how surprised, given that I'd been on medication to delay my labour. I explained to her about the young doctor with the Eastern European accent and asked her if she could find him so I could thank him properly. She didn't know who I was talking about, though, and neither did my husband or anyone else on the maternity ward.

To this day Teri has no idea who helped deliver her baby in her moment of need. All she knows is that without the intervention of that young doctor she might never have had the precious gift of her baby son.

Mandy didn't see an angel in the delivery room and neither was she offered help by a mysterious stranger, but she is convinced that angels are listening to her and watching over her family. Here's her remarkable story:

## 'It's a Miracle'

My first pregnancy was extremely difficult. I couldn't walk for long periods and needed to rest almost constantly. The last term was the hardest. There were many days when I would sit up in bed longing for the delivery date so that my ordeal would be over. I longed to meet my babies – I was carrying twins. During the last month or so of bed rest I spent most of the day praying that my angels would watch over the little ones inside me. I couldn't shake the feeling that something wasn't quite right, even though I could feel the little kicks inside me.

The delivery turned out to be every bit as tough as the pregnancy had been. Two hours into labour, the doctor decided that the stress rate of my babies was too high and I couldn't give birth naturally, as I had planned. I had to have emergency surgery. Our first son was born soon afterwards and when he was taken away to be cleaned up the room fell quiet and a nurse asked my husband if he wanted to leave the room while the doctor proceeded. I saw panic in his eyes and I knew that my second baby was in danger. Then I heard the doctor telling another nurse that our second baby had the umbilical cord wrapped around his neck. He was struggling to breathe.

After what seemed an eternity the doctor did manage to cut the cord, but my second baby didn't look strong. I blamed myself, because the doctor had wanted to proceed to surgery as soon as I had gone into labour, but I had been keen to try for a natural birth. Then I saw a nurse go over to the baby and lower her head. I started to cry. We were too late.

The doctor took the baby and placed him on a table. He wasn't moving and my husband was sobbing, but the strangest thing happened to me – I felt something like a bolt of electricity going through me. I can't explain it, but I had never felt so fit and energetic in my life. I prayed that my son would live.

Suddenly I heard a tiny cry from across the room and the nurse saying, 'It's a miracle.'

The following four weeks were full of highs and lows, but the angels stayed by our second-born son. He and his brother are now four years old, healthy and happy and full of life! They talk to angels every night and thank them for keeping them together.

Almost every mother feels that the birth of her child is a miracle but, as you'll see from Helen's story, the journey towards that miracle was a particularly traumatic one for her.

## Against All Odds

At 14 I was diagnosed with scoliosis and Marfan's syndrome. That was in 1978 and little was known about it then, but it affected my aorta and every year I'd have a check-up with a cardiologist.

When I was 20 and just married, I was told that it wasn't a good idea for me to have children. I was at extremely high risk of my aorta bursting during pregnancy, and if that didn't happen then it would during labour, and if by some chance it didn't then, it would within the first few years after the birth.

I hadn't ever really thought about having children before, but my sister-in-law had just given birth to her first baby and seeing her with that baby did something to me. During times when I wasn't working I would sit and knit little baby outfits for friends and even put some away for myself. It felt really silly collecting things for something I might never have, but I did it anyway. My sister-in-law had another baby, this time a girl, and the feelings within me deepened. Every time I went for a check-up I'd ask my cardiologist what he thought about the prospect of going ahead with my desire and every time he'd say that I was at extremely high risk of not making it through.

Nevertheless, after much soul searching I eventually made the decision to try for a baby of my own. When I found out I was pregnant I felt like a helpless child, not knowing what would happen. I'd pray for my child to be born healthy and for me to make it through and I asked my brother and sister to pray for me at times as well, as they believed in the miracle of healing. My cardiologist said there was no change in the test results and he only knew of one other woman with my condition who had had children and lived to tell the tale.

The odds were stacked high, but despite a difficult pregnancy and traumatic birth my prayers were answered when I had a healthy baby boy. A few years later, desperate to give my son a brother or sister, I fell pregnant again and delivered another healthy baby boy.

At that point I felt I had taken enough risks already, but then I fell pregnant for a third time. I nearly lost the baby at one stage during the pregnancy, but he survived, and I was convinced that his life was meant to be. He was the surprise baby I hadn't really planned on having, but he was wanted. For the first couple of days after he was born I would look into his eyes and he really looked as though he knew something he wasn't telling me. I'd never seen that look before.

I still don't know why I'm here to tell my story of hope while others are not. I've had some people insist I can't have been at that much of a risk, but I don't see it that way. I know what I was told for years and I also know that someone out there heard my heartfelt prayers and decided to organize things so that my wish could be realized. I believe that it was angels. So to people who see no possible way of having what they want, I would say that sometimes all you need do is believe.

## Brief Glimpses of Heaven

Babies are angels that fly to the Earth,
Their wings disappear at the time of their birth.
One look in their eyes and we're never the same,
They're part of us now and that part has a name.
That part is your heart and a bond that won't sever,
Our babies are angels, we love them forever.

**Anonymous**

Some people say that all babies are angels, and few first-time parents would disagree. Others say that when we are born our guardian angel kisses us just above the lips and below the nose – that's why we have a groove there called the philtrum. The word 'philtrum' is from the Greek word *philtron*, from *philein*, which means 'to love, to kiss'. Very fitting, huh?

There's a beautiful story in the Jewish Talmud which says that God sends an angel into a woman's womb when she is pregnant and this angel teaches the baby all the wisdom that can be obtained. Just before the baby comes out, the angel touches it between the upper lip and the nose and all that it has taught is forgotten. Similarly, in other traditions it is said that an angel shushes the baby in the womb to stop it from talking about heaven, or to make it forget about it, because if it were to remember too much it would never want to leave heaven and begin life on Earth. According to some vocal experts, the philtrum allows us to make a wide range of lip motions which enhance both vocal and non-vocal communication. Again very fitting, don't you agree?

The birth of a baby is a miracle in itself and reason enough to celebrate the presence of angels on Earth, but sadly not every baby lives long enough to begin their journey on Earth. The loss of their physical presence is traumatic and heartbreaking to those who have been eagerly awaiting the new arrival, but, as the stories below show, some comfort can be drawn from the fact that every unborn baby is reborn in spirit.

This beautiful story was sent in by the mother of a remarkable little girl and shows how children often have a bigger awareness of this life and the next than their parents.

## Alive in Spirit

A few years ago, before I even knew I was pregnant, my daughter was talking to her unborn little brother. I had an ectopic pregnancy and lost the baby at around eight weeks. Yet to this day my daughter still talks about her little brother in heaven. And we never actually told her that I was having a baby, or that the baby had died.

Then a little while ago she started talking about her baby sister and shortly after that I found I was pregnant again. When we asked her where her sister was, she said she was in my tummy. So then we asked when her birthday was and she said Christmas. Although we've known for a while now that I am pregnant, we only got our due date last week: 26 December.

It's interesting that for this little girl the fact that her 'little brother' died before he got a chance to live doesn't stop her talking to him. For her there are no boundaries between life and death. Her brother is alive in spirit and always will be.

Gail also believes that her daughter has a special connection with a sibling who died:

## Special Connection

I'm 38 years old now and have two beautiful children; my younger is my son Oliver and my elder is my daughter Jessica. Before I got divorced my ex-husband and I used to live in Bedfordshire. He is a policeman and before that he was in the army.

Once he got a posting to Northern Ireland. It was soon after we arrived there that I fell pregnant. Everything was going well until I was 22 weeks and then I started getting really bad pains. I went to the doctor and he said I had a water infection, so I thought that was causing the pain. Anyway he was wrong and two days later my daughter Courtney was born. The doctors didn't give any hope of survival, as she was so premature, but God love her, she was a fighter and lived for 25 hours, which, according to the doctors, was amazing.

We buried her in Maidstone in Kent and after the funeral we returned to Ireland. After that Jess, who was four at the time, started telling me that Courtney kept flying through her window to come and play with her. I thought it was very sweet that she was saying that, but didn't know whether it could really be happening.

73

She didn't talk about Courtney again until last week, when it was her fifteenth birthday. She told me then that she had seen her sister at the top of the stairs, but she said she only looked about five. I don't know what to think. Is it possible that they could be communicating in some way? I, too, would really like to have some sort of contact with Courtney but have had no signs whatsoever.

I replied to Gail and told her that not only was it possible that Courtney was communicating with Jessica, but that it was a reality. The reason Jessica saw Courtney aged five was because it was around the age of five that she last saw her in spirit. Courtney was simply reminding Jessica of that time in her life when she happily communicated with angels, so she wouldn't feel alarmed or threatened by her appearance.

I also told Gail that even though she feels she has no contact with Courtney, in spirit Courtney is with her every moment of every day and communicating with her all the time. She is alive in Gail's heart and spirit and also every time she looks into Jessica's eyes she will see Courtney. The bonds of love between a parent and a child are just too strong to be broken by death.

This intriguing letter sent to me by Michelle has certain similarities with Gail's story, but this does not make her experience any the less rare or special.

## 'With Us Somewhere'

Hello, I'm Michelle and I'm 38 years old and I'd like to share with you an experience which my partner of 20 years, Lee, and I had nearly two years ago.

It was around three o'clock in the morning when Lee woke up and told me he needed to spend a penny. When he got back he told me that while he had been in the bathroom he had happened to glance at the window and there, smiling back at him, had been the bright golden image of a teenage girl.

We were both really freaked out by this but I was happy at the same time because the only explanation for the appearance of this angel was that it was my daughter Natalie whom we had lost 17 years earlier due to premature birth. We had only had her with us for 26 hours and had both grieved for many years.

To this day I still haven't really got over it, but got great comfort from the fact that this visit could have been from her and that she could be with us somewhere. She was buried on 14 October and that was the date when the golden image appeared in the bathroom.

I think you will appreciate this next story, about a special little boy called Luke, which his mother sent to me via e-mail.

## Luke's Story

Fourteen years ago, when I was 23, I lost my little boy Luke when he was born prematurely. He only lived for eight hours. My world fell apart and it took me months to come to terms with his death. I felt totally alone. Although I was with his dad, and still am, I didn't think he felt the same loss as I did. Now I know that he just grieved in a different way.

Soon afterwards I was pregnant again. It was not easy. I could have lost the baby very early on and at one point it seemed there was no way they could keep my pregnancy going, but out of the blue my doctor told me that he was going to try something he had not done before. At that moment a feeling of calm and comfort washed over me. I knew that everything was going to be OK, and it was. In due course my son Kieran was born safely.

I always felt that is was Luke who guided Kieran into this world and over the past 13 years things have happened that have made me think that he is still looking out for him.

One day, for example, I was walking with Kieran to the school gate after a football match and, just as during my pregnancy, a feeling of calm and comfort washed over me. Kieran went to cross the road and normally I would have told him to be careful, but this time I didn't say anything, I just stood there looking at him. He started to run across without looking, then suddenly he stopped dead and turned around with a look of shock and fright on his face, narrowly avoiding a 4x4 that came speeding past.

Later that night he said to me that that he had felt as though he had run into a brick wall. At first he had thought that I had grabbed him and pulled him back, but when he had turned he had seen that I was nowhere near him. Some people would say this was just luck or chance, but I believe it was something else, as this was not a normal thing for a 13-year-old boy to say.

Kieran's mother asked me if it was her son's guardian angel or his brother's spirit that had pulled him back and kept him safe. I believe in spirit there is no distinction between the two. Our guardian angels can manifest their love, guidance and protection in countless different ways, including through the spirit of departed loved ones, even those we have never known in this life.

All the above stories were sent to me by women who lost their babies through miscarriage or stillbirth, but this next story, from a very brave lady I know called Sherry, tells a very different story.

## A Changed Life

I was a young girl, very young, when I chose to have an abortion. I had been dating a boy for a year and we intended to marry if I got pregnant. I thought I had everything planned out, so when I got pregnant I was so excited. But then everyone said I deserved to be a normal teenager and it would be better if I postponed motherhood until I had established myself in a career and my circumstances in life were better. Naïvely, I went along with it and believed an abortion would be the best thing for me.

Afterwards I tried hard to move on with my life. I hid the feelings of guilt, shame and relief – yes, I'm honest enough to admit that relief was there, as I really wasn't ready for the responsibility of a child – but I couldn't return to my life before I got pregnant because things had changed. I hadn't been prepared emotionally, spiritually and physically for what happened and I felt as though I had killed my baby. They say time heals all wounds but time went by and try as I might to lead a normal life, I just couldn't.

Six years later I was still searching for someone who would understand and help me, and this is when I met my guardian angel. In the meantime somehow I had managed to get through university and get my first job, but every night after work I would go home feeling empty.

I would go to bed and dream of my dead child. Waves of guilt would wash over me.

One night the pain and anguish seemed more acute than ever. I began to cry, as I had done for many years, but this time I also began to pray for help. A part of me felt I didn't deserve help because I had murdered my baby, but mercifully the stronger and better part of me prayed for strength and hope. Blinded with tears and feeling a vice-like pain in my chest, I prayed as I had never prayed before.

I'm not sure if I fell asleep or not, but what I do know is that a warmth came over me and when I looked up I saw bright stars in my bedroom. The anguish melted away as I saw an angel holding a baby in his arms. I couldn't see much of his face, as his hair was long and every time his wings beat together his hair flew in front of his face. Then I heard him say, 'This is your child. She is with us now and she has always been with us.' I found myself wondering what her name was and before I could ask the answer came, 'Her name is Grace.'

Since my vision I have found a perspective that has helped me think more clearly about the whole event and even talk to others honestly about my feelings of pain and shame. I don't think the regret will ever go away, but I have stopped suffering from bouts of self-hatred, guilt and depression and have started to feel human again, full of love and hope that I can share with others. It has taken me close to 15 years to heal the pain, but seeing the angel changed my life forever and put me in touch with a strength and inner peace and courage I didn't know I had.

Abortion will always be a painful and controversial subject. Many people write to me expressing their sadness over it and their sense of loss and tormenting guilt. They often wonder if their baby suffers in the after-life. But when abortion takes place, a spirit is not fully invested in a baby and returns to heaven. Sherry's story also shows that an abortion can occur for the mother's spiritual growth and, however distressing, can help her work through lessons of self-worth and learn to grow in self-love and self-enlightenment.

Dina's baby was stillborn and, as painful as the experience was for her, she also experienced something wonderful and today is convinced that it has helped her grow spiritually.

## Silent Night

The night after my baby was stillborn was the first time I felt an angel hug me. It is now eight years later and as I relive the tragic day in my mind, I know that it was my guardian angel who hugged me with love and comfort and that I am worthy of that love and comfort.

As the parent of an angel, I do not want to forget one detail of my son's existence or death. Connor was a very special little boy who brought many good things into my life through his passing. He was stillborn late in the afternoon on a Friday and I was placed into a room on a floor away from all of the happy new mothers. It was a ghost town with minimal staff and patients. I told everyone, including my husband, to go home. I wanted to be alone, to rest and think about what was really happening. I had no wires or tubes or anything hooked up to me, so there was no reason for me to be disturbed by nurses in the middle of the night. My room was quiet and as I melted into sleep I felt a pair of warm arms wrap around me and lift me slightly from the bed. I also heard the words, 'Sleep in heavenly peace,' and then, 'Silent night, holy night, all is calm, all is bright.' And that was how I truly felt. All was calm in my heart and all was bright for my sweet child entering heaven. And then my guardian angel helped me drift into the most wonderful and peaceful sleep.

## Just a Cloud Away

The loss of a baby through miscarriage, stillbirth, cot death or any other reason or under any circumstances is devastating. It is a shattered dream and a shattered reality. Parents have to deal with the loss of their hopes and with the loss of their child. This is no easy task. I hope the stories in this chapter have shown you that the loss of a baby is not an experience to hide or keep silent about or be healed by the birth of another child. Parents need to go through the grief process and feel what they need to feel before they can move forward with their lives.

Each baby that has died is a little angel just a cloud away. It was not their time to take their place in this world, for whatever reason. Perhaps they chose to give up this life and instead be reborn in spirit as a guardian angel watching over those who longed to see them on Earth. Perhaps they weren't quite ready for their guardian angel to kiss them and erase their blissful memories of heaven. Or perhaps, as I like to think, they just needed to linger a while longer in the love, comfort and joy that is life in spirit.

# Chapter 4

# Angel Children

'Perhaps children's innocence, wherever it comes
from, contributes to the fact that they seem to
see angels more often.'

**John Ronner**

If you ever need something to spur you on to a belief in
angels, ask a child. As you now know, that's exactly what
I did when researching this book. In the process I
discovered something I already knew in my heart but
had forgotten along the way, which is that children see
the miraculous in everyone and everything. Every day
for a child is an unexplained, inspiring and ever-new
experience, and within each of us, however old we are,
there is a child that has always believed in angels. So why
not take a moment to savour these heart-warming
stories about angels and children?

This first story was sent to me a few years back by
Leonard. It shows that for people who have had angelic

encounters in childhood, the experience will almost always retain its clarity and wonder.

## Sharing a Pillow

I was about nine years old, my mother and father had been separated for a few months and it was Easter time. I remember I was looking forward to eating lots of chocolate eggs after giving up chocolate for Lent.

One night when I went to my bedroom I saw a glowing white object lying on my bed. I wasn't scared – I felt excited and warm inside. The glowing object looked like an angel lying down with folded-up wings. I got into bed, just at the edge, and started to talk to it. Like most kids whose parents are separated, I wanted my mum and dad to get back together again, and I told the angel all about it. Then, when my eyes got sleepy, I offered it my pillow to sleep on. I fell asleep on my side at the edge of the bed so that the angel would have room.

A few hours later when my mum came up to bed, she woke me up and asked me why I wasn't sleeping right inside the bed. I told her that I'd given my pillow to an angel. She looked surprised and told me I must have been moving about in my sleep, but I told her this wasn't the case. 'Perhaps it was your guardian angel then,' she said, smiling. 'Yes, it was,' I replied, 'and I prayed for you and Dad to live together again so everything would go back to the way it was and I'd be happy again.' My mum didn't say anything, but hugged me tightly.

Although for years afterwards I slept on my side, I never saw my guardian angel again. One visit was all it took, though, because after that I changed. At the time my grades had been slipping and my mum had been called into school three times because of my bad behaviour, but after that she never had to go in again. She and Dad didn't get back together, but seeing my guardian angel made me realize that I wasn't alone and that my life was a blessing. I knew then that I needed to live it to the full.

Leonard has never forgotten the visit from his angel and he believes that it made him the individualist and successful entrepreneur he is today.

It's often the case that angelic encounters in child-hood are not fully understood at the time, but children are perhaps more comfortable with that state than adults. This was certainly the case for Karen:

## A Soft and Gentle Hand

When I was young, about five or six, my parents used to fight all the time. We lived in a small flat and they would argue either in the bedroom or in the kitchen, right outside my bedroom door. The door was usually left open a bit, as I was scared of the dark, so I could even see them squaring up to each other sometimes. It was always late, after midnight, when they had been drinking that I'd be woken up by the shouting. They used to say vile things to each other and there would be the smashing of glasses and plates and sometimes screams when they hit each other. It scared me and I used to lie there night after night putting my head under my pillow so I couldn't hear them. And I clearly remember on several occasions the touch of a soft and gentle hand on my shoulder. It would gently stroke my head and shoulder until I went to sleep. I never saw anyone, but I knew it was my guardian angel taking care of me.

Once I told my dad about my angel, but he screwed his face up in a nasty way and told me to stop talking nonsense. So I shut up about it and didn't dare tell any more grown-ups. It became my secret, a secret I haven't shared with anyone for 49 years. It's a tremendous release to share it with you. Just writing it down and thinking about the warmth and comfort my angel gave me has made me feel like a child again – not the scared child cowering from her parents, but a comforted and much-loved child.

My parents split up in the end. I lived with my mother and saw my father at weekends and things got better because they weren't fighting anymore.

Karen's story reminds us all of the love that angels have for children. In fact if you watch a child sleeping you'll see the reflection of the love of angels in its face.

Luke's story is another enchanting reminder of angelic comfort and warmth:

## Warm Blanket

I believe in angels. I saw one with my own eyes when I was about four or five years old. It is my first clear and vivid memory. I woke up from a nightmare where I was being attacked by flying dinosaurs and started to cry. I reached for my comfort blanket, but I couldn't find it anywhere. I didn't dare check the floor beside my bed as I was still scared from my nightmare. Peeping out from my covers, I saw a beautiful tall lady standing at the end of the bed. She had my blanket in her hands and started to glide towards me with it. I didn't feel frightened of her; she was so lovely and so gentle. I could see glittering wings behind her and she looked huge – over ten feet tall. I felt protected and loved. It was like drinking a mug of steaming hot chocolate on a cold winter's evening. She dropped the blanket on the pillow and then vanished.

Though I had my comfort blanket then, I never needed it after that. Somehow the warm feeling stayed with me and every time I felt scared or woke up from a nightmare I remembered it and drew strength from it.

People have often told me that I was just dreaming, but in my heart it was real. There was an angel in my room that night letting me know that I was loved and cared for and that I needn't be afraid.

Children need all the love and hugs they can get. They need to feel valued and appreciated, and if these needs are not met, life can be cold and difficult, as Kathy, whose story is below, knows all too well.

## 'A Voice Saved Me'

I was the youngest of five children and although I can't say I wasn't loved by my parents I never really felt that I was wanted. We never had much money and once when my dad lost his job I heard my mum say that they should never have had me because they'd just about been able to get by before. Thinking I was nothing more than an extra mouth to feed, I can remember days when I was engulfed by unhappiness. Looking back, the symptoms I was experiencing – tearfulness, apathy, a need to be alone and a lack of interest in anyone or anything – were those of depression, but at the time I just thought I was worthless. I often wished I'd never been born.

I had my first angel experience when I was eight. I needed to have some teeth pulled and was given a general anaesthetic. Things went dangerously wrong and

I nearly lost my life, but during the procedure I experienced something extraordinary. I found myself in a huge hall with high ceilings made of glass, surrounded by angels. It looked as though they were all eager to speak to me and all of them had something to say. I felt so overwhelmed by this I didn't know which one to turn to. I longed to be able to speak to them all, because they were all pouring light into me, radiating a feeling of warmth and love that I had never known before. It was intoxicating.

I woke up from the anaesthetic with that feeling glowing inside me. I was convinced it would never leave me, but as I grew older and tried to find my feet in the world it did grow weaker and finally the familiar feelings of depression and fear returned. Things reached a head when I was 16 and studying for my exams. I didn't have a clue about what direction in life I should take and was haunted by feelings of being unloved. Studying proved impossible and I dropped out of school.

It wasn't long before I drifted into a series of relationships with men who confirmed my feelings of worthlessness to me by abusing me either verbally or physically or both. It was after one particularly savage beating that one of my angels came to visit me again. I didn't see it but I heard it. I was cowering in the corner of the room, terrified that my boyfriend would set on me again. I closed my sore eyes and as I did so I heard a gentle voice saying, 'You need to get up now, Kathy.' I looked up, expecting there to be somebody else in the room, but apart from my boyfriend there was no one there. Then again I heard the voice: 'Kathy, you need to get up now.'

Shakily, I got to my feet. My boyfriend instantly got up to confront me, but there must have been something about me then because for the first time he looked scared. I walked straight past him and left his life for good. I thanked the angel for remembering me and giving me the courage I needed.

Five years have passed since then. I went back to my studies and qualified to go to nursing school. I've not been in a relationship since, but I have friends who love and protect me. Like a lot of abused women, I once lived in a hostile world in which bad things happened and there were no angels watching over me. The world I live in now is very different. I see angels all around me and best of all I see the angel within me.

Kathy's story touched me very deeply. Her childhood was clearly a very unhappy one but with the help of her guardian angel she has quite literally been able to get to her feet and find her way out of the darkness into the light. Most important of all, she feels fulfilled and enriched and her inner angel shines through today for everyone to see.

Feelings of love, protection and safety also shine through this next story, which was told to me by a woman called Elaine:

## 'A Feather Brushed my Heart'

I would like to share with you something that happened to me many years ago when I was ten years old. I was at my mother's funeral, sobbing hysterically. My mother had been killed in a car accident on her way to pick me up from school and I blamed myself for not offering to walk home from school like the other kids.

My uncle and aunt tried to comfort me at the funeral, but I didn't want them near me. I must have been creating quite a scene, as I remember my uncle saying that it might be best if he took me home. At that moment a feather dropped down from somewhere above me and landed on my knee. We were in church, so I don't know how it got there. A while later I felt a tingling sensation at the back of my neck and it grew until I felt it all over my back. The tears and guilt that I never thought would stop flowing melted away and I sat quietly.

Near the end of the funeral I began to feel a presence behind me. I closed my eyes and felt warmth, peace and love. Though my eyes were closed, I could see an angel standing there. It was surrounded by very bright white light and was much bigger than I was. I felt it wrap its wings around me and gently, so gently, kiss my cheek. It was a beautiful experience and one that I drew strength from in the years ahead. Whenever I missed my mother, I remembered the angel hugging me and somehow my loss became easier to bear.

Drawing strength and comfort from angelic experiences is a familiar theme in the stories that have been sent to me. It's hard to describe in words, but from personal experience an encounter with an angel feels as though the sky has opened and an arrow of light has cut through the darkness. In this state of loving, trusting conscious-ness we understand that angels are real and they live within us as well as outside us.

Rediscovering this forgotten reality feels like a slice of heaven on Earth. It's something we dream of and long for, but don't experience enough. Even if we only manage to live in this state of love and wonder for a short while, memories of it can help us build a bridge from our earthly life to heavenly thoughts, feelings and experiences, from loneliness, pain and suffering to joy, peace and love, and then to the angel in ourselves and the angels in others.

Angels also push us out of ourselves into a world of love and goodness and show us that when we base our decisions on love it is impossible to lose our way. If things aren't working out in our lives and we feel alone, lost and afraid, perhaps it is because we are not as open-hearted or as receptive to their loving guidance as we could be. If the angels find the doors to our hearts closed, they will not force an entry. This is once again something that children can teach us. They have the ability to trust the angel inside them and to see angels all around them, even when they feel vulnerable, scared and in need of rescuing.

## Angelic Protection

Childhood can be a very risky time. Unaware of the possible dangers, a child will dive into a river or run across a road, and although parents, teachers and carers always try to keep an eye out for potential danger, it is not always possible. Fortunately, protection of the vulnerable is a common theme in angelic encounters, like this one reported to me by Jacky:

## Flying Backwards

I was driving down a winding country road one evening to visit my sister, who had just had her second child. The light was failing so I drove at a steady, safe speed with my sidelights on. I was coming up to a sharp curve in the road when a van came up very fast behind me. The driver was obviously in a big, big hurry. He kept trying to pull out so he could overtake me. I know I shouldn't have done it, but when the nose of his car was virtually on my back bumper I stuck a couple of fingers up at him. He hooted his horn in anger and then started to overtake me at great speed.

Shaking my head and swearing under my breath, I looked back at the road ahead and saw a boy coming from a path on the right side. He was looking the wrong way down the road and it didn't seem to occur to him to check the cars coming in the other direction. By now the van overtaking me had seen him too and started braking, but there wasn't enough time and space for him to avoid hitting the kid.

My heart seemed to jump into my throat and everything went into slow motion. It was only then that the child turned his head towards us and that was when something amazing, bizarre, strange happened: I saw the child jolt into the air and then fly backwards onto the side of the road. It looked as though something invisible had lifted him up and pushed him to safety. He didn't jump, but his feet left the ground and the overtaking car missed him.

I stopped and jumped out of my car to check that he was OK. He was a bit shaken up, but there were no injuries. The man in the van didn't get out, but at least he stayed long enough to see that the boy wasn't hurt. I wish he had got out, as I would dearly loved to have discussed with him what I had seen. I wondered if he had seen the boy fly too. I asked the boy himself to describe what had happened, but he said he couldn't remember anything apart from falling backwards into the road.

Jacky knows in her heart that this was something far more than a lucky escape.

In another car rescue story, Declan is also convinced invisible forces were at work:

## Steering Wheel

Last November I went to collect my girls – Lily, aged five, and Connie, aged two – from the child minder. I parked the car in front of the house, which sits halfway up a steep street. After picking the girls up I strapped them both into the back seat and then got behind the steering wheel. I was just about to drive off when Lily let out one of her ear-piercing screams: 'Daddy, Daddy, I forgot Bubble!'

Bubble is a soft toy dog; Lily bonded with it at birth and simply can't live without it. I sighed, opened the car door, closed it and hurried back to the house. I was only gone a minute or so, but when I returned the car wasn't there. It was rolling down the street and picking up speed. There was a junction at the bottom of the hill and there was no telling what might happen. I ran down the hill screaming. I'm a fast runner, but the car was going too quickly for me to catch up with it. I could hear my girls screaming for me. It was the most terrible moment of my life.

Then, still running behind the car, I saw it gradually move towards the pavement, bump along a stretch of grass and decrease in speed until it crashed over a dustbin and stopped. I pushed the back door open to pull out my girls. They were freaked out, but absolutely fine. It was a miracle.

Later, when I put Lily to bed and tucked her up with Bubble we talked once more about the incident. It was then that she told me that she had seen the front wheel gradually turning further and further, as if someone was steering it off the road. 'Do you think an angel was driving?' she asked me. I had no idea what to say. But from the perspective of a devoted dad, there was no other possible answer.

In much the same way, Zack is 100 per cent sure about what happened to him. It took place 40 years ago, when he was five.

## In the Arms of an Angel

My grandmother promised me she would always watch out for me when she died. When I asked her how I would know she was there, she would say if I wanted to see her I should look at the stars – she'd be twinkling up there among them. She died just before I started school and I was happy to think that she was up in the stars.

On the night before my first day at school, I found it hard to sleep. I guess I was worried about leaving my mother and being away from home during the day. In the past when I'd felt nervous or worried about anything Grandma would always have calmed and reassured me with her loving words, so I decided to get out of bed and talk to her in the sky. It was a very cold night but the stars were out in all their glory. I sat for a while by the window in my bedroom thinking about Grandma, but then I decided that my window wasn't high enough. There was a window in the hall that was very high. Bursting with excitement, I grabbed a chair and climbed onto the sill and pressed my nose against it.

I'm not sure exactly what happened next, but somehow I lost my balance and fell backwards onto the hard floor. I didn't hurt myself in any way, though, because instead of falling I felt myself being carried by a pair of soft and gentle arms and placed gently on the floor. By then my mother was on the landing looking angry. I told her what had happened but she didn't really listen. She just guided me back to my bedroom and told me I needed to sleep as I had school in the morning.

The next morning I woke up and instead of dreading school I couldn't wait to begin my new adventure. When I walked onto the landing I noticed that the chair was still there, proving I hadn't imagined it all.

Forty years on I can remember that night in every tiny detail and no one is ever going to convince me that an angel didn't lift me in its arms.

It's often said that every child has a guardian angel and as we've seen there is plenty of evidence to suggest that angels do indeed have a special interest in children. This is because children are more vulnerable and perhaps need more protection and guidance than adults. This is not to say that angels look after adults any less carefully than they look after children. But perhaps children are less rigid in their thinking and more likely to recognize an angel when they meet one.

## Living with Angels

There are also, it appears, some children who not only see angels but live alongside them.

About five years ago I got a letter from a psychiatric nurse called Sheila, who had been working with mentally challenged children for 24 years. She told me about one 12-year-old girl in her care who talked to angels all the time. This girl said that the angels kissed her when she was upset and watched over her. Sheila asked me if perhaps in similar ways to the deaf and blind developing other senses, the mentally challenged develop an extra sense or bridge to heaven.

Since then I've had a number of letters from parents or carers of children who suffer from mental and physical disabilities. Here's one of them, which was sent to me by a lady who preferred to remain anonymous:

## Special Glow

My daughter suffers from mental illness and we care for her 24/7. She will be 13 next year. Last winter we took our eye off the ball and she wandered out of the house. We could not find her for five hours and it was terrifying. I had visions of her wandering into the road or hooking up with horrible people who would take advantage of her disability.

Then, as the light began to fade, she wandered back up the garden path smiling. She told me that an angel had found her, held her hand and walked her back home.

I've received numerous moving stories from parents who have witnessed glows or light around the beds of children who are disabled in some way or suffering from a terminal illness and this has convinced them that angels are watching over them. It has been an enormous source of comfort to them. Some may say this is nothing but wishful thinking, but I know in my heart that the parents and carers who have told me about these things have been speaking the truth. And, from my observations of the children with disabilities and misfortunes that I've spent time with, it would certainly seem that they have been blessed with angelic dignity and the ability to express love.

The ability of angels to apply emotional balm to children who are disabled or suffering in some way is well documented, and this is also the case for children who have been victims of physical abuse, like Tyrone, who writes:

## Castle on a Cloud

My childhood was one of beatings – horrible, savage beatings – by my parents and older brother. I was the family scapegoat. My life was miserable during the day, but at night angels appeared in my room and told me how special and important and loved I was. I was abused for ten years, but my angels never left me and encouraged me to focus on my schoolwork. I'm glad they did, because I got the grades to be able to leave home for good.

## Where was the Love?

After reading these stories you may wonder, as many people do, myself included, why every innocent child is not protected from danger by their guardian angel or given hope and inspiration as these children were. High-profile abuse cases such as the horrible tragedy of Baby P spring to mind. Where were the angels for these beautiful children? Where was the compassion? Where was the justice? Where was the divine intervention? Where was the love?

When she was 13 a friend of mine lost her mother to cancer. She had been sick for ten years. My friend sat with her regularly during her final summer of struggle. Her hair fell out, her body wasted away and her mind came and went, often leaving her unable to recognize her own child. Years later, when my friend found out I was writing about angels, she got in touch with me and told me straight how angry she was that angels hadn't been there for her or her mother. If angels did exist, she said, how could they allow such terrifying physical and mental degradation to happen to such a wonderful woman and for a child to witness it all and be scarred emotionally by it? She told me that after her mother had died she had stopped believing in a higher power completely. She didn't think that there was any use for prayer or talk of love when the memory of returning daily to the horrible caricature of her mother was burned into her mind.

Almost all of us have been confronted by some equally sad and painful situation in our lives and have probably asked why angels allow bad things to happen to good people or innocent children. The problem of human suffering, especially to the young and innocent, is, I believe, the biggest obstacle to belief in guardian angels. If our guardian angels really care for us and can intervene in our lives and move mountains, why do they permit us to suffer? Why don't they cure cancer and other terrible illnesses? Why don't they end terrorism, cruelty, natural disasters and child abuse? It seems impossible to reconcile the loving power of angels with a world where injustice, misfortune, suffering and cruelty often gain the upper hand.

The answer to all of this is that there is no answer. Both good things and terrible things will happen to us for reasons that we will never fully understand while we are in our human form. Perhaps in spirit we will get the bigger picture that we need to fully understand these events, but until then we need to come to terms with the fact that life is filled with very real suffering, as those who have lost a loved one, seen their marriage fail or had their life torn apart by some other terrible misfortune will know only too well.

These things are a part of life, and suffering is part of the human condition. We may wish that this were not so and there are countless books that trade on that hope, dispensing advice on how to think, eat, pray and behave in order to avoid suffering, but suffering will come just the same. In spite of our best efforts, the world we live in is an uncertain one and impossible to control. The only thing we *can* control is the way we *respond* to suffering and, as the stories in this chapter have shown, for some people, misfortune, depression, tragedy and loss can lead to greater spiritual awareness.

Like the pain of labour before the joy of birth or the darkness before the dawn, suffering can open our minds and hearts to the angels inside us and all around us. It can show us that the only thing we can really be certain of and trust and depend on in this uncertain world is the awesome power of love. Love is eternal and unchanging and stronger than death. Love works to unite rather than divide us. Love is the ultimate power and the only truly effective weapon there is against suffering, hate, injustice and cruelty. Love is the only language that angels speak. And the more we choose to welcome angels into our lives and centre our lives around love, the more powerful the force of love becomes and the weaker the forces of darkness become.

## Stop!

Let's return now to this chapter's theme: the timeless love angels have for children. My extensive research has shown me that angels can appear to children in all shapes, forms and sizes. Children seem to see what they can cope with. While a soft, glowing light or sweet smell can comfort some, others cope extremely well with a full-blown vision complete with wings and halo. For some children a voice is all they need to guide them, like seven-year-old Adam in the story below.

## 'The Voice Told Me'

I was walking Adam, my nephew, home from school. He was seven at the time and a bundle of energy and noise. I loved to hear him chatter, but that day I was preoccupied. I had my driving theory exam the following day and a lot of information was swirling around in my head.

Adam noticed how absent-minded I was and tugged on my arm. Apologizing, I made an effort to concentrate. I asked him what he had most enjoyed about school that day. Delighted to have my full attention, he launched into a monologue about his favourite topic: the playground zombie game. He had tried unsuccessfully to explain the rules to me many times before but was perfectly happy to explain them all again. I tried to concentrate, but my eyes must have glazed over because Adam suddenly shouted, 'Stop, Aunty Sara, stop!' There was such urgency in his voice that I stopped walking and knelt down beside him, worried that he might be ill or in pain.

Moments later a car swerved onto the pavement and plunged into a fence. In an instant it dawned on me that if we had continued walking it would have hit us. The driver got out, clearly dazed. I could smell alcohol on his breath. Soon he was joined by an angry home-owner wanting compensation for a crushed fence. As a witness, I gave my details and then hurried home with Adam.

On the way home I asked him if he had seen or heard the oncoming car. Was that why he had shouted that loudly? 'No,' he replied in a matter of fact way, 'the voice told me.'

I really believe he has a guardian angel.

I have no doubt that an angel intervened and spoke through Adam just in time to save him and his aunt from being struck by that car.

About five years ago a woman called Rina wrote to tell me about a similar experience she had when her son was one, but on this occasion the angels inspired – even commanded – her to help her child herself.

## Voices from Heaven

I put my one-year-old baby son down in front of the window so he could watch his dad cutting the grass in the garden and sat down to make a phone call, but as I was dialling I heard a voice saying, 'Get away from the window.' The tone of the voice was so urgent that I couldn't ignore it. I put my mobile down and picked up my son and just as I moved away from the window a cricket ball flew through it at great speed.

Glennyce's story is equally remarkable:

## 'A Voice in my Head'

I woke up in the middle of the night feeling agitated. A voice in my head was telling me to get up and check my three-month-old son.

I ran to his bedroom and found him pinned underneath his crib. The bottom had fallen out of it and it had collapsed in on him. I pulled him out and he was fine, but I dread to think what could have happened if I hadn't got there when I did.

## Intuition

Was it coincidence or something else that alerted Rina and Glennyce to the danger involving their children? Both women believe that 'mother's intuition' was the source of the mysterious information. Intuition means knowing something without the use of reasoning or the five basic senses and I believe it is the voice of our guardian angel speaking. When there is a strong emotional bond between two people, like that between a mother and a child, intuition tends to be at its most powerful because, as mentioned previously, love is the language that angels speak and wherever the bonds of love are at their most powerful, angels cluster.

We are all born with intuition and have all had experiences involving it, even if we don't think we are intuitive. For example, a common occurrence is to think of someone we haven't seen or heard from in a while and then shortly afterwards, out of nowhere, this person shows up in our lives. Many of us have dreams while sleeping and then shortly afterwards find ourselves in the same situation in waking reality. Another common experience happens when we are out, for example in a shopping centre, and feel a pull to look in a certain direction. Then we turn and lock eyes with someone who has been admiring us from a distance. Of course, they often look away quickly when they realize they have been caught!

Throughout time, many of the world's most accomplished artists, musicians, writers, scientists, engineers, philosophers and world leaders have based their decisions on their intuition – or on hunches, insights, visions, sixth sense and gut feelings, which are simply other terms for it. What these people have really been doing is working with the angel inside themselves. They have listened to their inner angel and allowed it to fly without limitation. But it is not just high-achievers who are capable of rising above the ordinary. We are all capable of genius if we learn to recognize that all of us are gifted – and the invisible guardian angel inside us is our gift. And if we all listened to the voice of that inner angel, we would become more like angels ourselves and make Earth a little more like heaven.

Children are born with their intuition highly developed. Recognizing and responding to it is something they do instinctively and naturally, even if adults doubt or question them, as they did in Megan's case. Her incredible story was sent to me from Australia by her grandmother Melissa.

## Finding Peter

My daughter Lucy got hooked on drugs when she was 14 and still at school. I was oblivious, partly due to the fact that she had always had behavioural problems. When she started having mood swings and problems with teachers, I tried to home school her. It was a disaster. I didn't have the patience to give her what she needed.

When she was 16 she fell in love with a boy and it got pretty serious. She ended up pregnant and he broke her heart when he left her a week after the baby was born. This began the downward spiral into total drug addiction. Her mood swings became so bad that I was scared she would get worse if she stopped taking the drug she was addicted to. She had fits and rages and started to shoplift to buy drugs. Two or three times a week I would have to pick her up from the police station after she had been arrested. I was out of my depth and blamed myself. I was scared, helpless and at my wits' end, and now I also had a granddaughter, Megan, to look after. She seemed to be the only good thing to have come out of all of this. Lucy seemed lost to me and, rightly or wrongly, I focused my energies on the baby.

Three weeks before Megan's second birthday Lucy left home and I'm ashamed to say that I was relieved. I was out of money, energy and hope. Treatment option after treatment option had failed and when Lucy had asked me to take care of Megan until she got clean I had agreed. She promised to stay in touch, but in spite of this she soon disappeared and lost all contact with her daughter.

Taking care of Megan wasn't easy, as I'd had Lucy in my early forties and becoming a mum again in my sixties wasn't something I'd planned on. I love Megan dearly, though, and couldn't imagine life without her.

One morning when Megan was almost four she bounced up to me and told me that I had to find Peter, her baby brother. I told her that she didn't have a brother, but she insisted that she did and that an angel had come in the night and told her to look for him. At first I dismissed what she was saying as fantasy, but she kept on with it all through the day and finally I began to wonder if perhaps she was somehow telling the truth. It was certainly possible that Lucy, wherever she was, had had another child.

The next morning Megan seemed to have forgotten all about her baby brother, but I hadn't. I decided to call the maternity wards in the local hospitals. There was no record of Lucy in any of them and I was about to give up when a voice inside my head told me to keep trying. I phoned some hospitals in the next town and eventually discovered that Lucy was in one of them. She had given birth to a baby boy three days before.

When I visited Lucy in hospital she was angry and defensive. She asked me how I knew she had given birth. When I told her what Megan had said she started to cry and told me that the reason she had stayed away was that she was ashamed of herself. She still wasn't clean and so once again I stepped in to take care of her baby. She hadn't given him a name yet, but in my mind there was no other name for him but the one his big sister had already given him: Peter.

Melissa's story is an awesome illustration of how the angelic in children can ignite the angelic in adults around them.

This story below about six-year-old Chloë, sent to me by her dad Stephen, also shows how watching children listen to their angels can encourage us to look for our own.

## Making Sense

One Saturday I was driving Chloë to her swimming class and we were talking about birds. I'm an avid bird watcher – the feathered kind – and she asked me why I enjoyed it so much. I told her that birds were beautiful creatures with wings and watching them made me feel peaceful and happy.

'You mean like seeing angels,' she said.

I wasn't sure what to say to that, but before I could reply she told me in a very matter of fact way that she could see angels. I'd never spoken to her about angels before and neither had my wife. We weren't into that kind of stuff. I asked her when she saw angels and she told me it was just before she went to sleep. An angel would sit on the bed with her.

Later that evening I tucked her into bed after reading her a story. She was surrounded as usual by soft toys and I joked that there wouldn't be room for her angel to sit down now. She started to move about in bed, squinting her eyes and muttering to herself. I wasn't sure what was going on but eventually after a few moments she told me that I was wrong and her angel was sitting on the bed. Humouring her, I asked her what her angel looked like. 'Like anything I want her to,' she replied. I asked how she talked to her angel and she said, 'It is like pictures and thoughts and feelings.' Then she said that her angel was an old friend of my angel.

I asked if I could speak to her angel. She paused and then said that her angel wanted to know why I needed to talk to her. I replied that I was interested and wanted to learn. This seemed to be good enough because I was urged to ask away, and ask away I did, with Chloë acting as a go-between me and the angel.

The first questions I asked were simple and fairly trivial – for example I asked if the angel had wings and lived in heaven. The answers I got were formulaic – angels can have wings and heaven is their home – but then Chloë went on to explain that heaven lived inside everyone. This seemed a remarkably profound thing for a six year old to say. I went on to ask more insightful, testing questions then, such as what advice the angel had for me and Chloë, and each time I was astonished. It was not Chloë's imagination that surprised me, as children have fantastic and agile minds, but the quality and maturity of what she was saying. I would ask a question, she would pause and then, in simple, elegant words, reply with the kind of insight about life rarely seen in adults, let alone a six-year-old child.

From our conversation I got the idea that Chloë's guardian angel did not so much solve problems or make life easier for her as provide a kind of bigger picture of the issues involved, a clarity and life wisdom that helped to centre, calm and comfort Chloë. She did not hug Chloë physically, but reminded her that she was loved.

When my daughter isn't speaking for her angel she is a typically giggly and gorgeous daddy's girl, but that night she was a profound and perfect angel interpreter.

I know it is possible that my daughter has wisdom and insight beyond her years and there is no way I can verify the source of her inspiration in a scientific way, but what I can do is observe her, and in the five years since we have had that conversation – and many others – I have seen her consciously tap into a well of insight, wisdom and love. And watching my child make sense of her life by finding her own source of knowledge and comfort has reminded me to rediscover my own.

Children are naturally intuitive and, if encouraged by supportive parents like Stephen, naturally insightful. I have learned from experience over the years not to pretend in front of my children. They can see through it right away and sense when I am feeling angry or hurt. It's uncanny. There is just a quiet knowing between me and them. I suspect it is the same for most parents. Lara wrote to tell me about her intuitive daughter.

## 'It Will Be OK, Mummy'

Ever since the age of five my now seven-year-old daughter has been walking up to me and laying her hands on my head when I'm about to get a migraine. She often knows when I'm going to get an attack before I do and has soothing words to say like 'It will be OK, Mummy.'

I'm sure many other parents and carers have had similar experiences when their child's instinctive response has been proved right or when they have shown wisdom beyond their years. From the moment they first enter the physical world as newborns, babies rely on their intuition for communication and protection. In a similar way to animals, they rely on these primary unspoken impressions for their physical daily survival at a time before their language, mental and social skills have developed.

So whether you call it intuition or an inner angel, children of every culture, religion and race are born with it. There are millions of very normal intuitive children playing, working and dreaming with the help of their angels all over the world today. They play in city streets, on the fields of farmlands or in suburban backyards. They are poor and rich, black, white, yellow and brown, short and tall, male and female. Physical background does not limit their special abilities. Each child's ability to listen to and work with their inner angel is as natural to them as loving, learning and breathing.

There's a lot of talk these days about so called indigo, crystal or star children. According to this theory many children born since the 1970s are old souls and have come into this life with special spiritual skills. There have been many books written about these children, giving details of their talents and how to raise them. The idea is that these special children will remind us of the long-forgotten healing techniques of psychic awareness and immeasurable compassion. While there is much wisdom in the little ones of today, all my research on children and angels suggests that in the eyes of angels, all children, not just a select few, are naturally gifted and have much to teach us about living life in the now with energy, passion, trust, imagination, spontaneity and intuition, whether they claim to be able to sense angels or not.

Children aren't perfect or faultless – far from it, as perfection is an unnatural state where no change or growth is possible – but while we may try to teach them all about life, more often than not it is they who teach us what life is all about. And perhaps the greatest thing of all that they can teach us, as the next chapter shows, is that there is always more magic and possibility in this life than meets the eye.

Chapter 5

# Invisible Friends

'Imagination is more important than
knowledge. Knowledge is limited.
Imagination encircles the world.'

**Albert Einstein**

Next time you are in the company of a three-year-old
child, just watch. Suppose the child is holding a small
cardboard box in their hand. One moment they will be
talking to you, the next they will be rushing off to play
because their special friend has arrived. The excitement
draws you in, but you can't see anyone. Ignored by the
child, you sit back and watch a spectacular game of planes,
trains, cars or dolls take place with a cardboard box. Before
your eyes you witness a transformation from the physical
world into a world of magic and possibility. Is this child
taking you innocently into the world where imaginary
friends come from? Are they having their first spiritual
connection with angels, the universe and beyond?

A recent survey suggested that as many as one in five children have imaginary friends. Here's what a few parents had to say when they found their household mysteriously expanding:

## Always Room for More Friends

When my daughter Sara was about four, her imaginary friends Ruby and Rachel were always with her, especially when she was being told off for something she said she hadn't done. It lasted until she was about five, so a whole year. I'm surprised she had imaginary friends, as she was the youngest of four children, but she still had time to play with them.

**Anthony, father of four**

## Don't Sit on my Friend!

When Mark was about one and a half he started to play with someone who was invisible. The first time I noticed it was when he pointed to an empty chair and said, 'Baby'. When he got older he said his friend's name was Monica. We had to be very careful not to upset Monica by placing bags or, worse still, ourselves on the chair that Monica was sitting on. I never worried about Monica because Mark was always happy when she was nearby. He doesn't mention her anymore – he's six now – but at the time she was very real to him.

**Sonia, mother of two**

## 'Angel on my Shoulder'

My daughter is in her twenties now, but when she was a toddler she used to hold her hands out to be picked up by someone who wasn't there. As she got older she would also hold out her hand as if it was being held. When I asked her about it she used to say it was Grandmother Joyce, who had died when she was a baby. Some people might be spooked by something like this, but it makes me feel better knowing that perhaps Grandmother Joyce is still watching over us.

**Nina, mother of one**

As we've seen previously, children are very receptive to angels and spirits, whereas adults often aren't, so is it possible that these friends are something more than imaginary?

Sadly, I can't draw on my own childhood to answer that one. I never had an imaginary friend when I was growing up. My friends were my dolls, my teddies and the toy soldiers I adopted when my brother grew out of them. I'd talk to them endlessly and set up tea parties and games for us to play together, but I always knew there wasn't really anyone there.

However, my son did have an invisible playmate, a pirate called Bill, when he was about three or four. It lasted for about a year and stopped when he started school. Whenever I talked to him about Bill he would look to the side and answer without thinking, as though he knew this friend very well. He told me that Bill was a kind pirate, not a bad one, and that he was 18 years old. He also gave me other details about his clothes and hair without batting an eyelid. It seemed as if he could see Bill and hear him talking back to him.

I often wondered if Bill was my son's guardian angel and since then, the more I have gathered stories like the one below, shared by Georgia, the more I have started to consider it a very real possibility that a child's imaginary friend *is* their guardian angel.

## 'Pay Attention Please!'

I was a very energetic child. It was hard for me to sit still in class and concentrate. I didn't know why I was like that and why other children could understand words and figure out numbers on a page so easily when to me everything looked like a rash of dots and lines. When I was in the fourth year of my primary school I remember spending more time outside the classroom than inside it, and when I was inside it I remember spending more time gazing out of the window and daydreaming than trying to work out what was written on the board.

One morning after I'd been sent outside the classroom again for not paying attention I felt particularly wretched. I knew my parents were worried about me and I was worried too. Why couldn't I learn like the other kids? Why couldn't I sit still for long enough? Why was my mind always somewhere else? I got angry and punched the wall behind me in frustration, then when my energy was spent I sat down with my back against the wall, held my head in my hands and started to cry quietly.

It was then that I heard a voice speaking right behind me. It seemed to be coming from the wall I was leaning against. It wasn't a male or a female voice but it was the kindest voice I had ever heard. It told me not to worry and that everything would be alright and that I would learn to pay attention.

Slowly a feeling of comfort crept over my heart and I felt as if the voice coming from the wall was my friend, a friend who knew all about me and loved me just the way I was. I turned around to face the wall, but there was no one there and no one standing beside me. Yet I could still hear the voice telling me there wasn't anything wrong with me and everything would be fine. I also felt a hand gently but firmly touching me under the chin and lifting my head up.

This wasn't the only time I heard the voice or felt the gentle hand lift my head when I felt low about myself. It happened on many other occasions after that and always quietened me down and boosted my courage and self-belief. I even started to look forward to hearing the voice. Sometimes I would talk to it in my head and whenever I did I felt it close by.

With my invisible friend beside me, life was never the same again. The following year my teacher suspected that I had attention deficit disorder and taught me to do my homework in different ways. She gave me extra help and my parents did too. My only regret about it all is that the more help I got from my parents and teachers, the less I heard from my invisible friend until eventually it vanished altogether. Yet I shall never forget that calming voice and the reassurance it gave me. I believe that my guardian angel had come to tell me that whether I paid attention in class or not, I was still loved.

Andrew also has special memories of his guardian angel coming to reassure and comfort him when he needed it most.

## The Lady in the Curtains

My dad was in the army and there were long, long periods when he wasn't around. When he was back home, Mum was happy, I was happy and life just seemed to have more colour, but when he wasn't around there was always a hint of sadness and tension in the air. I'd create a calendar every time he served overseas and count the days until he came back. And then one day he didn't come back. There had been an accident in training and he'd sustained injuries to the head. He died five days later.

When my mother told me that Daddy was in heaven, I stopped breathing. I wanted to be absolutely sure this wasn't some terrible nightmare, so I held my breath until I nearly passed out. My mum panicked and grabbed me and the two of us just howled with grief.

Everything about my world changed. Everything I did and everywhere I went brought back memories of Dad. I'm 55 years old now and it still hurts when I think back. I was only eight then and Dad was the centre of my universe.

It was the night after I had heard that he had died that I first saw the lady in the curtains. Exhausted with crying, I remember lying in my bed with my mum holding my hand, staring at the curtains. There were swirly shapes on them and wearily my eyes traced around them. Then I closed my eyes and pretended I wanted to go to sleep. I wanted Mum to go so I could be alone to pray for Dad to come back to me. Then when she had tiptoed out of the room I opened my eyes again and when I did I saw a lady come out of the curtains. She was smiling at me and there was bright light all around her.

'Listen to me, Andrew,' she said in a lovely voice that sounded shimmery and beautiful. 'Your dad has asked me to come and tell you that he loves you and is never far away. He had to go away suddenly and there wasn't time for him to say goodbye or to let you know how much he loved you. But I'm here to watch over you and to remind you of your dad's love for you and how proud he is of you. He is relying on you to help your mother while he is gone. Alright?'

I was too stunned to say or do anything that night. I just stared at the lovely lady until I drifted off to sleep. All the next day I couldn't stop thinking about her. She appeared again the next night and the night after and I began to look forward to seeing her and hearing about Dad and how much he still loved me.

The lady in the curtains also helped me out when I went to secondary school and got a crush on a girl called Isabelle. Try as I might, I couldn't talk to her, but when I told the lady about it she laughed and told me to ask Isabelle to help me with my French homework – she was brilliant at French. I plucked up the courage and did as the lady said and Isabelle was every bit as lovely and as kind as I'd thought she was. Nothing much came of it, but I'd made the breakthrough and talked to a girl. Then school and social life took over and frequently I was going to bed so late and so exhausted that I wasn't awake enough to speak to my friend and over time she just melted away.

When I had finished my GCSEs and was applying for the sixth form my mum told me how very proud she was of me and how my love and strength had helped her get through losing Dad. I didn't say anything about my friend, as I didn't think she would believe me. She told me how proud Dad would have been of me as well and as a present gave me a montage of photographs she had made of me and him together from the day I was born until the last time he was with me. I looked at the photographs with tears welling up in my eyes and then one of them caught my eye. It was a picture of my dad in my room – which was a nursery then – with me in my cot. He was standing by the cot smiling at the camera and pointing at the curtains. I asked Mum why he was doing that and she told me that she'd chosen everything for the nursery because Dad had been away, but he'd insisted on buying at least one item and that item had been the curtains. I'd sometimes wondered why Mum – who was very house proud – had always insisted on dry cleaning my curtains instead of buying a new set and now I had my answer.

So what was going on here? Was it coincidence? Was it imagination? Was Andrew reading much more into all this than was really there? Stories like this one do seem to stretch the mind, but I have collected many that are similar during the course of my research.

Karen e-mailed to tell me about her daughter's invisible friend. Here in her own words is her extraordinary story:

## Oisin

I went through a horrific relationship, but it gave me two lovely children and my faith back. The nightmare didn't end when my relationship did, though. I lived in constant fear and was getting over 40 phone calls from my ex at different times during the day.

My father was my best friend while I was going through this, but he hadn't always been, because when I was growing up he had been an alcoholic and there had been violence in the house. When he was given three days to live we took him to a rehabilitation centre and it worked – he stopped drinking. Afterwards he told me that he should have died but he had been sent back to make amends and he did. He had been off the drink and the cigarettes for seven years when he was told he had cancer.

Even though my dad was terminally ill, my life was peaceful at this time. I loved living on my own and I loved my children and they loved my father too. It was around this time that my little girl had an imaginary friend she called Oisin.

My father wanted me to meet a man who treated me with respect, but I told him not to worry about me and said that if he was still worried when he got to heaven, he should send someone lovely to me. He said that he would.

A few months before he died I went to church and a fellow came in and sat behind us. I didn't really speak to him, but afterwards my daughter told me he was Oisin's daddy. Sometimes I would give her sweets in church to keep her quiet and from then on whenever I went to church and offered her sweets she would always ask me to give Oisin's daddy a sweet. At the time, because of my past experience with men, I got my mother to give him a sweet instead.

My dad died in March and I think my son must have sensed something, because he woke up screaming at five past four that morning, moments before I received the phone call with the sad news.

After Dad's death I felt very low. I still went to church and my daughter still wanted me to give 'Oisin's daddy' a sweet. Then one evening when I was out with friends, I bumped into him and he started talking to me. I found it hard to talk to any man at that time, but because I knew him from church I felt safer. I thought he was married, as he wore a wedding ring, but his wife had died, leaving him with two children.

Today we are together and guess what, we have a wee boy called Oisin! I still find it funny that my dad told me he would send someone to me and that my daughter's imaginary friend Oisin brought us together.

This story could be explained as an attempt by Karen's daughter to find a partner for her mother, but what a successful attempt! Actually, I'm not sure which strains belief more – Karen's daughter's superb matchmaking skills or her very real 'make-believe' friend. With so many other true stories about children whose invisible friend plays with and occasionally helps them, I know what I believe.

I know, though, that there are plenty of people who would disagree with me. Psychologists argue that invisible friends or mysterious helpers in childhood exist only in a child's imagination, but just because you can't see, hear, feel or touch something doesn't mean to say it isn't real. Some parents believe that a child introduces an imaginary friend into their life because they are lonely or lacking something. Others say that it is a phase. But there is also the very real possibility that the child is actually seeing someone adults can't see.

According to the laws of physics, there are many things in our world that we can't perceive with our human senses but know are there. For example, televisions work because waves you can't see send and receive messages that translate into a picture. It's the same for your mobile. You can't see the frequency that allows you to speak to someone miles away, but you know that it is there because your friend talks right back to you. Many scientists now agree that existence is multi-dimensional and what we see, hear and feel isn't all that there is. Seen in this light, it is very possible that some children, young children in particular, with receptive minds and hearts have the ability to perceive realms of existence that adults can't.

Moving on to the next batch of stories, you'll see that it is not just guardian angels that children can see and communicate with but other manifestations of the world of spirit. An imaginary friend can be a soul who isn't incarnate and who hasn't completed the full transition to the other side. Often children speak with grandparents or other relatives who have passed on or someone who was very close to them.

Here's Grace's story:

## A Pinch of Salt

I had several miscarriages and each one affected me deeply. My grandmother was upset, too, as she was long-ing to have a great-grandchild. She was also very worried about me, though, as her younger sister had died in child-birth and her elder sister had become seriously ill and almost died during her pregnancy. She survived, but her baby was born with severe handicaps and needed round-the-clock care. So when I announced that I was pregnant yet again I wasn't sure how my grandmother would take the news. Instead of looking anxious, though, she just smiled and told me that the pregnancy was a blessing and the reason why things happen as they do would become clear to me one day.

When I started to bleed in the early days of my pregnancy I was confined to bed. I suffered the foulest morning sickness, but eventually passed the magic three-month mark. I'd never made it past ten weeks before. Something was different about this pregnancy, I could just feel it.

When I was about five months gone my grandmother fell ill and within weeks her condition was critical. My mum stayed with her and I visited when I could.

When I was 34 weeks I had a terrible scare – I thought I had gone into labour. I was rushed to hospital, but was told that everything was fine. When I got home, the saddest news was waiting for me on the answerphone: Grandma had died. Heavy with grief and heavy with child, I carried my baby for another four weeks.

Monica – named after my grandmother – was born healthy and beautiful and she had the largest pair of eyes I had ever seen on a baby. They immediately reminded me of my grandmother's eyes. When she was two years old she was in the kitchen with me one day when I was baking some spaghetti bolognaise and she just came out and said, 'Pinch of salt'. I asked her what she meant and she told me that the nanny who looked after her at night always told her that everything tasted better with a pinch of salt. I remembered Grandma always saying that to me when I was a child and I was so shocked that I dropped the bolognaise sauce bowl on the floor. Monica howled with laughter.

About a week later when I was doing the housework Monica asked me to play some beetle music. Slow to catch on and thinking about insects, I didn't know what she meant at first, but when I questioned her she told me that her nanny liked to hear the Beatles. Then it dawned on me that when she did the housework Grandma always used to play the Beatles. Intrigued, I asked Monica to tell me about this nanny. She told me that she was a 'funny lady' with 'the bestest smile' and was her 'special friend' because they had the same name and were born on the same day.

There were more instances like this which convinced me that Monica was communicating with her grandma. It all stopped when she was about six. I'm not sure what it means, as obviously grandchildren are going to resemble their grandparents in certain ways, but at the time she seemed to know things about Grandma that I had never told her. Also, she was born in September and my grandmother was born in March, so they weren't born on the same day, although I guess you could say that Grandmother's death was a kind of birth in spirit?

Grace admits that she isn't sure what to think, but I wrote back to tell her that despite all the questions and uncertainty she feels, one thing is crystal clear from her letter: in one way or another her grandmother lives on. And her story is a beautiful reminder that our departed loved ones can live on in our children's eyes.

Some children are clearly close to the world of spirit from birth, or in Erol's case before birth. Erol's mother told me that he first spoke about his 'other life' and his 'friend in heaven' at the age of three and a half.

## 'My Friend in Heaven'

One day Erol shocked me by telling me that before he came to be with me he was with Grandfather Eron. His grandfather's name was Eron, but Erol couldn't have known that, as my father had died over 30 years before and I'd never spoken to Erol about him. Erol told me that the place he came from was warm and light with lots of fields and other boys and girls waiting to be born like him. He also told me that there were big people there who looked after them and Eron was his favourite because he used to make flowers that could sing with him. My father had been a florist.

There were too many coincidences for me to think that this was just a child's vivid imagination. When I took Erol to the seaside for the first time he squealed with delight and told me just before he had been born he had swum in a sea like this. Erol had taught him some strokes. My dad had insisted I learn to swim from an early age because on one occasion he had nearly drowned, so again this sounded just like him. Even more amazing was that as soon as Erol started swimming classes he showed no fear at all of the water. His teacher said he had real potential and took to swimming quite literally like a duck to water.

As Erol has grown older, the stories of his other home and his time with my dad have become fewer. Now he's six years old he seems to have forgotten them, but I am certain that he knew my dad in spirit and had some memories of his life before birth.

Many children seem aware of layers of existence that quite simply confuse or astonish adults. Being fresh from heaven, the possibility is strong that they are more open to memories of their lives before birth as well as to contact with spirits and angels. The huge volume of letters I have received over the years and the vast number of websites and books devoted to the subject of children with mediumistic or psychic abilities certainly seem to suggest that more and more children have the ability to connect with the world of spirit. Alternatively – and just as exciting for me – it could suggest that more and more parents are allowing their children to express their psychic gifts instead of shutting them down by telling them that what they see, sense or hear isn't real. In other words, children are no more or less gifted psychically than they have ever been; the change has been in their parents' response and encouragement of their psychic gifts.

Other amazing 'I see dead people' stories about children as well as adults can be found in later chapters, but here we'll move on to a couple of stories about children who appear to have been visited by angels in human form. Let's begin with this story faxed over to me five years ago now by a lovely lady called Maria.

## Lost and Found

When I was young, about four or five, I remember being taken to a fairground by my grandparents. We did the rides first and then I got my candy floss. Then we started to wander around the other attractions. My grandparents got engrossed in one of those impossible throwing games where you try to win a prize by throwing a hoop over it, and while they were preoccupied I got it into my head that I should watch the people on the big wheel. I really wanted to go on it, but I was too young.

I had every intention of heading there and coming straight back, but things didn't work out that way. The big wheel was further away than I thought, but I finally got there. After watching people screaming for a while I got bored and decided to go back to my grandparents. I must have taken a wrong turning, though, because I ended up near the bumper cars.

It's terrifying when you are a child and you are lost. I thought about trying to find where the car was parked in the car park, but that meant leaving the fair and crossing over a road and my grandparents would be really cross with me if I tried to do that myself. So I just stood there, frozen with panic.

Then a kind-looking woman came up to me and asked me if I was lost. She had piercing blue eyes, a white dress, a blue shawl and a matching blue bag. I started crying and she took my hand and led me to the entrance to the fair. I saw my grandparents there looking terrified and as we got there the woman told me that I should run over to them quickly. This was peculiar, as I hadn't told her who they were or that I was at the fair with my grandparents that day. When I got to them and told them about the kind lady they wanted to thank her, but even though we looked, she was nowhere to be found.

This can be easily explained in that it is possible that this kind woman saw me earlier with my grandparents and put two and two together when she found me crying and alone. At the time, though, my grandmother said that lady was my guardian angel and I believed her. It was incredibly comforting for me to think that I had someone watching over me when I needed help.

By the time I got married myself and had children of my own I had stopped believing in angels. The lady in the blue shawl had simply been a kind woman doing a good deed. But when my son was four, something similar happened. I took him to the zoo and while I was paying for some candy floss, he wandered away. Panicking, I started to run around frantically looking for him. I ran up behind a lady to ask her if she had seen my child.

When she turned around, I swear it was the same lady from all those years ago. She had the same blue eyes, blue shawl and peculiar blue bag, and hadn't aged at all. As before, she seemed to know exactly what my problem was without me telling her anything. 'He's gone to see the lions,' she said softly, pointing me in the right direction.

I didn't hesitate and rushed over to the lions, where I found my son staring at the enclosure with his thumb in his mouth, oblivious to the panic he had caused me. I hugged him tightly and told him to never ever wander off like that again.

Maria's faith in guardian angels was renewed after her experience at the zoo. She felt comforted by the knowledge that when she really needed help, that kindly lady was close by.

Gary too remembers being helped by a mysterious stranger, even though he was very young at the time. His story is fascinating not just because it is another illustration of an angel in human form being there at exactly the time when a child needed it most but also because it wasn't until he was out of danger that it occurred to him that there was a problem.

## Going Home

One day when I was about six and a half I missed the school bus home. It was my fault because I'd drawn a picture of our house with Mum and Dad and me smiling out from the windows but had forgotten to collect it, so I'd gone back to the art room to get it. When I got back to the front of the school, the bus had gone. I didn't want to cause any trouble or for people to think I was stupid, so I decided to walk home. It was only about a mile or so.

I headed off walking. I knew where to go, so I didn't lose my way, but what I had forgotten was that there were a number of busy roads to cross. I'd learned my green cross code, so I thought I could handle it. I crossed the first road successfully and with my confidence growing by the minute I attempted a second. I wasn't so sure how to cross this one, though, as it was a much bigger road and the traffic was travelling quickly. I noticed an island in the middle of the road and decided to head for that. I waited for a break in the traffic and made a mad dash for it. Once on the island, things looked even tougher to navigate, but just as I was about to wait for another break in the traffic, a man grabbed my hand. He was dressed all in brown and had red shoes on. He looked kind, so I didn't feel alarmed, and I let him help me cross the road safely. He told me that it was brave and clever for me to try and walk home on my own but these were busy roads and in future if I missed the school bus I should tell one of the teachers to phone my mum or dad and ask them to collect me. Then he helped me across another busy road and walked with me down to my street. When my house was yards away he shook my hand and told me that I could take it from there. I thanked him and ran to my door. When I looked back to wave at him, he had gone.

My mother opened the door and her eyes were red and strained. She'd been so worried when I hadn't got off the school bus that she'd called the police. I showed her the picture I'd painted for her, but she shouted at me and then hugged me so tightly I couldn't breathe. Until then I had no idea that anything was wrong.

Gary often wonders who that man in brown was and how he knew where he lived. Perhaps he was just a kind person who had seen him about or perhaps he really was a guardian angel protecting a child from harm?

## Mysterious Strangers

People who don't put much stock in talk about angels believe that mysterious strangers are just that – kind people who happen to come along at the right time to lend a helping hand. Yet there remains something compelling about them and there are often a number of reasons why the children (and adults) who experience them remember them as remarkable: they arrive and disappear virtually unseen; they often have knowledge of events, names, places and people that they couldn't possibly know; and they often have exactly the right tool or remedy for the crisis at hand. All these characteristics suggest that something extraordinary is occurring.

If these strangers are angels there is no need to explain the miracles they perform, but if they are people then how is it possible to account for all the strange things they know, say and do? Are they perhaps guided, either consciously or unconsciously, by a higher realm to a situation where their skills can help? Many of the stories I've received about this phenomenon seem to suggest one or all of these possibilities. Certainly, whether human or angel, these remarkable people seem to be out there – and perhaps one of them could be you!

But how many of us in this current climate of paranoid parenting would hesitate before helping a child or offering advice and companionship? Stories about mysterious strangers helping children remind us all of a time when the world seemed a safer place and it wasn't considered a crime to befriend or offer a helping hand to a child you didn't know.

For a few months after the toddler Jamie Bulger was murdered, some supermarkets displayed a poster showing a close-up photograph of an adult clasping a small child's hand. The caption beneath it said: 'Don't let go, it only takes a second.' In the years that have followed we have witnessed an escalating fear of the uncontrollable freak event – the stranger taking a child. Indeed, the recent responses to the events surrounding the disappearance of little Madeleine McCann have led to a further escalation in the fear of unknown individuals who could be lurking anywhere.

It is a sad and terrible fact that isolated incidents of child abduction do occur and we should all be vigilant as far as our children are concerned, but it is also important to get a sense of perspective. With little hard evidence or data, the news media emphasize the dangers of internet predators, convicted sex offenders, paedophiles and child abductors, suggesting that the problem is extensive without putting it into context. The truth is that the risk of a stranger harming a child is extremely small. Children are far more likely to be harmed by people they do know, or to be killed by accidents in the home or on the roads than by strangers. Yet despite this, 'stranger danger' remains our biggest fear and children are being denied the freedom to play and trust adults as a result.

I remember when I was a child I would spend hours wandering alone in the park or woods, climbing trees.

Today's children have little or none of the freedoms I enjoyed. More and more children are being cocooned at home and denied the experiences that their parents enjoyed in terms of exploring and interacting with their peers. In addition, the consequences of 'stranger danger' fear are damaging to the relationships between children and adults, creating a society based on fear rather than trust.

People are susceptible to the scaremongering around children because we live in a society that has lost faith in itself and in which people are losing faith and trust in each other. Of course we want our children to be safe, but we also want them to be happy, healthy and well adjusted, and to do this we need to trust each other a little more, especially as far as our children are concerned. I sincerely hope that reading the stories in this book, especially those about mysterious strangers, or, as I like to call them, 'angels in disguise', will restore some of that faith and trust.

As Jan's story seems to suggest, even if a child can't see, hear or feel it, their guardian angel is always close by:

## Invisible Guardians

Every morning on my way to work and every evening on my way home from work I pass a busy primary school. In the morning it's always crowded with children, parents, cars and bikes. In the evening it's a lot quieter. By the time I walk past, which is usually around 5 o'clock, most of the kids have gone home, but there are always a dozen or so still waiting to be picked up, with a teacher in charge constantly looking at their watch. I feel a bit sorry for them but I know how it is when you're a working parent. When my kids were at school I used to try as hard as I could to pick them up in time, but then the phone would ring as I was leaving my desk or there would be a pile-up on the motorway and I'd be late.

As it tends to be the same kids staying late at the school and as I walk past them each day, I have started to recognize their faces. In recent weeks, though, something really peculiar has started to happen: I have become aware of older kids in the playground, kids I didn't see at first, one with each of the little children. At first this struck me as odd, as the school only goes up to the age of seven, but I thought perhaps it was some kind of play scheme. The next day when I passed I saw the older children again and stopped to get a closer look. It was hard to make out what they looked like, because try as I might I couldn't focus on them for very long. It also looked as if the younger children didn't see these children. Even odder was that when a parent arrived to collect a young child, the older one following them just wasn't there anymore.

I don't see the older kids every night but I have seen them often enough to be convinced that they are the children's guardian angels watching over them until their parents arrive to take them home.

I could go on and on with stories about children and their guardian angels, and you'll find a few more of them scattered through the rest of the book, but it's time to move on now and explore how angels watch over us at all stages and ages of our lives, from teenage years to adult-hood, old age, death and beyond. Before that, though, I'd just like to talk briefly about the importance of nurturing imagination, creativity and intuition in children.

## Nurturing Intuition

Intuition, as I've already mentioned, is the ability to sense what cannot be explained rationally and is the door to the world of the unseen. It seems to flow in children because it feels natural to them and children do what feels natural. But sadly, all too often a child will state very plainly to an adult what their experiences are and if that adult is not experiencing the same, they will dismiss what the child is saying. In some cases, that child will interpret this as indicating that what they are seeing and hearing is not normal, and as a result they will begin to see, hear, sense and feel less and less.

So, how do you go about developing your child's intuitive nature? If your child senses something you don't, listen sympathetically, neither praising nor scolding. If they start talking about an imaginary friend, treat it just like a new schoolfriend. Ask your child simple questions about their imaginary friend – their name, their age, where they were born, etc. – and listen to their answers. Remember, children learn fear. They are sponges and everything you say is incorporated into their belief system. Phrases like 'This isn't real' or 'It's all make-believe' can lead to beliefs that are limiting and these boundaries can hinder their intuitive abilities and psychic growth.

Parents, teachers and carers have an amazing opportunity, just by listening, asking questions and being open with children, to expand their own world as well as the world of the children in their care. Whether we are young or old, imagination and the creativity and intuition that spring from it are truly important. Without them we are earthbound, but with them we can fly. With just a little intuition and a splash of imagination, our dreams can really come true.

In my opinion all children should be encouraged to listen to their intuition and be informed of the reality of the guardian angels who watch over them. Think about it: how would your childhood have been different if you had known that no matter what happened you had a guardian angel standing next to you and that you were never alone? How much more confident would you have been if you had known you had an angel on your shoulder, encouraging you to take risks, grow and learn and appreciate how special you were? Now think about how different your teenage years would have been if you had known an angel was telling you that your potential for happiness and fulfilment was limitless. And what if your guardian angel had reminded you that the reason you were on Earth was to make a difference in the world? How would your life have been different if you had known that a being of light was by your side, whispering to you that your dreams could come true and that the only thing in your way was your fear and self-doubt? How precious would you have felt knowing that your guardian angel was always watching over you?

Any child and any adult will benefit greatly from re-establishing their relationship with their guardian angel and rediscovering the magical possibilities all around them. And, as you'll see from the astonishing stories in the next chapter, all that our guardian angel needs from us is the willingness to trust the still, small voice of love, goodness, trust and hope within.

Chapter 6

# 'Take Care of this Child'

'I went forth to find an angel
And found this effort brought
That life is full of so much good
The touch that angels wrought.'

**James Joseph Huesgen**

Based on reports throughout history it seems that children do perceive the spirit world and angelic beings more easily than adults, but we don't need to lose that special connection with angels when we grow up. In fact, with an open mind and heart, it can grow even stronger.

As children we all had the instinctive ability to listen to the angel inside us. This angel is not physical and doesn't grow old, and however old we are it will forever be young, like a playful and divine child. So there is still a child in each of us that has always believed in miracles and when we rediscover this child, we realize there is great hope. It hasn't been that long and we haven't really grown old at all.

So sit back and let the stories in this chapter remind you of something you once knew but may have forgotten: that in the eyes of our guardian angels we are all children in need of love, protection and guidance.

## Guardian Angels

This first story wasn't sent to me but was widely reported by the media in January 2009. Perhaps you'll remember reading it?

### Saved by the Voice and Hand of an Angel

A British survivor of the New Year's Eve nightclub fire in Bangkok said that an angel dragged him to safety when he was overcome by smoke. Twenty-nine-year-old Alex Wargacki was with seven friends when he saw the fire start in the three-storey Santika club at around 12.30 a.m. on New Year's Day. With the exits blocked by panicking crowds of people, Alex was overcome by smoke and lost consciousness.

The fire went on to kill dozens of people, but Alex was not among them. He was quoted as saying: 'I woke up and heard this voice saying, "Come on. Come this way." Then I felt myself being dragged towards an exit and then

I was out in the open air. Had it not been for the voice with the hand of an angel I would not be alive.'

Alex admitted that it was possible a fireman or someone at the club saved him, but he couldn't be sure.

Many people believe that each of us is assigned a guardian angel at conception and this angel doesn't disappear when we leave childhood behind. It stays with us through adulthood and is with us when we depart this world and enter the next.

Our guardian angel does what it can to make our life run smoothly. Sometimes this is by inspiring a thought to spur us into action, at other times it is by lending us super-human strength, as in the case of a woman who was able to lift a car long enough to free her trapped child, or by influencing events, for example when a runaway truck with an unconscious driver at the wheel inexplicably swerves at the last moment to avoid a bus queue of people. Or, as happened with Alex, an angel appears to save us from danger. In fact, there are many instances which are put down to luck, coincidence or even miracles that have the touch of a hand of light behind them. This was certainly what Joyce felt when she reached one of the darkest and most dangerous moments of her life, coincidentally also on New Year's Eve. Here, in her own words, is her story:

## Fenced In

Several years ago I was going through a really bad period in my life and, seeing no way out of my depression, I decided to end my life. It was New Year's Eve, my birthday, about 4.30 p.m., when I went to a reservoir on the outskirts of the town where I lived. It had a path round it wide enough to take a vehicle. The distance round the path was about a mile and there was a six-foot fence separating it from the water.

I stood on the path, contemplating the enormity of what I was about to do, and then decided to get on with it. As I stepped towards the fence, I heard footsteps approaching from my right and a man appeared out of the mist and passed behind me. I turned my head slightly to look at him and he glanced at me with what I thought was a faintly disapproving look and then carried on into the gloom and disappeared.

I gave him time to get well out of sight and then once more I went to the fence. As I did so, I heard footsteps from my right again and, turning, saw the same man with the same look of disapproval on his face. I decided it really couldn't be the same person and again let him walk on.

But as I tried to go for the fence for the third time, the man appeared for the third time.

Now completely unnerved by the experience, I gave up and went home.

It's possible that the man Joyce saw was simply a concerned member of the public, but, angel or not, his presence was nothing short of miraculous because it stopped her from doing something terrible.

So why don't guardian angels come to our aid every time? Again I've lost count of the number of times I've been asked this. Sometimes it seems that angels must stand back, giving loving support only, as we work things out for ourselves. These are the times when we feel alone, the dark before dawn. But if we can work through these dark times and discover the angel inside us, life is never the same again. Here's Ann's remarkable story:

## A Prescription for Happiness

It's over a year now since the birth of my first child, a daughter, and I have never felt so light and joyous. I can see angels and magic all around me. After 20 years of struggling, I've finally learned why I always felt different.

I'd always thought I was mentally unstable – not a great asset when you consider that I'm a registered nurse, so I didn't talk about it to anyone. But I can't remember a time when I wasn't on medication of some sort or in and out of hospitals for breakdowns.

After giving birth to my daughter I noticed no postpartum depression, but clearly my doctor was aware of my higher than normal risk. Drugs were prescribed and I was urged to stop breastfeeding in case they were passed on through my breast milk. I didn't want to stop breast-feeding, but then October came and clouds were rolling in and the days were getting darker. I tried to ride a high of new-baby happiness and pretended to my health visitor that I was absolutely fine. But I wasn't. I was depressed, exhausted and tense. I was seriously losing perspective. I had to do something.

My husband wanted me to take the drugs, but I had no idea how they would affect me and my ability to care for my daughter. Every drug I had taken in the past had made me unbearably sleepy. They had also drained all the feeling out of me. There was no way I wanted to go back to that. I remember calling a friend to babysit while I ran to the library. Looking up a book about coping with depression, my eyes fell on seasonal affective disorder, and I immediately knew that was my problem. I visited a specialist the next day and started a course of treatment.

You may not see my turnaround as a big deal. But I had been fighting the depression in my head with very poor medical support for 20 years. You may wonder how it was that a nurse didn't see the blindingly obvious and I don't really have the answer for that except to say that perhaps I believed there was a fault in my upbringing and personality. There were no lab tests, CAT scans, X-rays or ultrasounds that could tell me what I had. So, if it could not be measured, in my mind it had to be my fault.

It was my daughter who really got me to take a long hard look at my life and the patterns of depression that were controlling it. When she was born I realized that to take the best care of her I also had to take the best care of myself. She is truly my guardian angel. Her birth has brought me my own health and given me the gift of happiness.

Ann didn't see an angel, but her daughter put her in touch with her inner angel and her life was transformed as a result. Her experience isn't uncommon. Many people discover angels in this way and the feeling of exhilaration and strength they gain from knowing that they are stronger than they believe themselves to be brings a sense of magical possibility into their life. Others, however, do believe they have actually seen an angel.

## Seeing Angels

Full-blown angel sightings are incredibly rare but they do happen and I've been fortunate enough to receive letters about this phenomenon from people like Sylvia:

## Kind Faces

I often see angels. I see them when I'm about to fall asleep or when I am just waking up. Sometimes I see just one angel but at other times there are several of them sitting in the chair or in the corner of the room or standing next to my bed. They have kind faces and there is one who is always there. He has silver hair and a silver beard and I think he could be my guardian angel. I smile when I see them and they smile back. I'm often too sleepy to speak to them and I either fall asleep and they are gone or wake up and they disappear. I've been told that at the moment when you are falling asleep or waking up you are more likely to see aspects of existence that would otherwise be invisible, and that is what I believe.

Sharon was 16 when an angel appeared and changed the direction of her life:

## A Change of Course

I was in the middle of a course I wasn't enjoying and was unhappy and worried, but didn't know what to do.

One night I was lying in bed worrying and close to tears when I saw something out the corner of my eye. I looked at it more closely and saw the golden outline of someone kneeling by my bed. I looked away and back, amazed, and the being was still there. It eventually went away and I lay awake for a while longer, but I wasn't worried anymore. Soon I fell asleep.

I woke up the next morning knowing what I had to do. I left the course and started on one more suited to me. I am enjoying the path I chose now, caring for children, and don't think I would have been here if it hadn't been for the being guiding me. I believe that's what he/she/it was doing.

Jonathon also believes he saw an angel:

## Rising High

In June 1981 I was 13 years old and that was when I saw my angel. My mother had died in the April of that year and 16 June was her birthday. On that day I went with my dad to the cemetery so we could lay some flowers on her grave. While Dad was staring at Mum's grave I turned around and found myself looking at an angel in the sky. It was about the size of a tall building and seemed to glow like a diamond light-bulb, only it was brighter and more beautiful. It was dressed in a long white gown that covered its feet and had huge wings tucked into its back. It had a book in its hands with silver light glowing from it. The light was too bright and intense to tell if it was a male or female angel or to see any features on its face.

To this day I don't really know the significance of this visit and when I told my dad I don't think he believed me. I often think of it, though, and it makes me feel warm and happy when I do. I remember everything from that day as clear as crystal. I didn't imagine it.

Without exception all the people who have contacted me to say they saw an angel share Jonathon's conviction. They sincerely believe they were not dreaming or imagining it. Paul is 100 per cent convinced...

## 'I Saw an Angel'

I saw an angel. I know I did. I know what I saw.

When I was about 15, I was staying with my grandmother for the summer. One night I was in bed and I don't know if I was awake or asleep, but I felt the need to roll over, and when I did there was a woman standing there in white. She wasn't really glowing, but I could see her well. I couldn't see into her eyes, however, and as a matter of fact the whole incident happened so fast, it is hard to say what did happen. The memory of it has stayed with me my whole life, though, and convinced me that there is more to this world than we can see.

Louise is also 100 per cent convinced. Here's her experience:

## Angels in the Clouds

One evening I was driving along a small country road. I had decided to avoid the motorway as it was a beautiful day and I wasn't in a rush. I was heading towards the sunset and there was a thunderstorm moving in from the north. The combination of the two natural phenomena created a stunningly beautiful sunset. I stopped the car and stepped outside to get a better view and only wished I'd brought my camera.

My attention was instantly caught by a patch of grey cloud drifting in from the north, illuminated by the rays of the fading sun. I swear to you that in those clouds I saw a host of angels. This wasn't a case of vivid imagination. Even though they were so far above me, I could see every detail of their faces. I could see their hair and their wings. They looked a lot like humans but had a glow about them. It was as if they were using the cloud vapours to reveal their beauty to me. It was so real and so true. It wasn't my imagination.

Often in letters like this one the writers repeatedly tell me that it wasn't their imagination. It is clear that when they have shared their stories with others they have repeatedly been told that what they saw wasn't real. But, as mentioned earlier, the question of what is real and what isn't real is something that even scientists struggle to answer. There are layers of existence invisible to the human eye and who is to say whether or not these people are glimpsing other realities?

So far many of the angels described have appeared in rather surreal forms. Suzanne's story is an intriguing one in that her angel took a recognizable human form.

## Meeting Edel Quinn

When I was in my late twenties I had a tremendous experience which changed my life. I was hitching a ride one day when a lady stopped to give me a lift. We had a very interesting conversation about spiritual matters and during the journey she gave me a prayer and on the prayer was a picture of Edel Quinn, who had passed to spirit in 1944. She was a remarkable and inspirational woman who worked with the poor in Africa for many years. I was happy to accept this prayer.

When I arrived at my parents' house I found out that they were planning to sell up. I was really upset, as I loved the family home. They told me that they had keys from a local estate agent for a property they intended viewing in the morning.

That night I went to bed feeling very upset. I decided to pray to Edel Quinn before I went to sleep.

It felt as though I had barely slept when I suddenly woke and there at the side of my bed was Edel. She was hovering above the bed with a heavenly light around her. She looked the same as in the photo. She smiled at me and then within seconds she was gone.

I felt scared and turned on the light. Seconds later I felt a sensation like hands pressing down on my head. At that moment I felt a peace and calm descend. I sensed they were the hands of Jesus.

The next day my parents decided not to sell and gave the keys back to the estate agent. I knew then that Edel's smile had been a smile of reassurance that everything would be OK.

Often angels will speak to us through people, images and memories that feel reassuring and comforting to us. In Suzanne's case her guardian angel spoke to her through a vision of Edel Quinn and her faith in Jesus, but although angels can choose to speak to us through our religion, because they respect what is important to us, they are not tied to any particular religion or belief system. They never bother about whether a person is religious or not, or even whether they consider themselves spiritual or not. For them there is really only one path to heaven and that is love. The moment we choose love, angels can lift us up to find heaven.

I'm including Mick's story here because it has something important to say about angels and the preconceptions we may have about them:

## The Bag Lady

To be honest I have had a number of experiences which I now confidently attribute to angels. On this particular occasion I was driving past a layby near Ewell in Surrey and was intending to stop and buy a mug of tea. I spotted a bag lady sitting nearby and felt a surge of compassion. I thought I would buy her something to drink and maybe to eat. Then suddenly I realized I had forgotten to bring any money with me that day. I felt so disappointed that I could do nothing for her. As I drove past I had a clear look at her. She had quite strong features, wore loose wraparound clothing and had a shawl wrapped over her head.

As I drove on to my next call (I'm a sales rep), I wondered how she had ended up there at the side of the road with nothing but her clothes and a few carrier bags stuffed with belongings. Did she have a family? Did they know of her plight? Did she have any brothers or sisters?

As I was musing on these questions, I passed a lady walking along the pavement. She almost looked from a bygone age in her elegant long black overcoat, sensible shoes and hat. She was very upright and slim and walking at a brisk pace in the same direction that I was driving. As I passed her I glanced at her face and was amazed to see that she bore a striking resemblance to the bag lady I had just seen. I was astonished and could only wonder if they were sisters.

Shortly afterwards, still conjecturing on what I had seen, I arrived at the newsagent's in Ewell. I entered the shop and asked if the owner was around. I was told he would be with me shortly. I turned round and, to my astonishment, standing outside and looking directly at me through the window was the very smart lady in the long overcoat and hat. I thought, 'How can that be her? There's no way she could have walked that far in the time.' She continued to stare at me and I was mesmerized, thinking, 'Does she really look like the bag lady or is it just me? Is it the bag lady or the bag lady's sister or what?'

All these thoughts were spinning around in my head with no answer for what seemed an age but was probably only ten seconds or so. It was certainly a long enough time for two strangers to stare at each other, though.

Then I had my answer: the lady turned her head to her left and, incredibly, slowly hunched over and morphed into the bag lady. It was like a sophisticated computer-generated image changing from one thing into another. Needless to say, I was transfixed. I probably had my mouth open!

At that point the shop owner appeared and started talking business to me. Of course the next time I looked, the bag lady was gone.

I found the whole thing inspiring and it has changed the way I think about people and life in general.

Although many people who write to me share Mick's firm belief in angels, and an angel sighting or encounter, however unusual, simply confirms that belief, there are also those who write to tell me that until they had their angel sighting they had never really thought about angels before. Marnie was one of those people.

## Wake-up Call

I'm a pharmacist and quite a functional person. I do believe in something, but I wouldn't say I was religious or spiritual in any way. I always believed that when a person got ill it was medication, not love or spiritual mumbo jumbo, that would help them.

Anyway I got the wake-up call of my life on the morning of 19 March 2007. I was sleeping alone in my flat when I was woken by a tugging on the bed covers at the foot of the bed. I've always slept with my bed covers pulled right up to my neck, so the tugging annoyed me. I was vaguely aware of it but then drifted off to sleep again.

Then it happened again. This time I sat upright in bed and looked at my alarm clock. It was 5.11 a.m.

Then I saw a beautiful girl standing about a foot away from my bed beside my cupboard. There was a white light surrounding her head and her hands. She wasn't facing me, but was gazing out of the window.

I rubbed my eyes to check I wasn't dreaming. When I looked again, she was still there. I wasn't frightened at all and took the time to look at her properly. She was wearing a graceful white dress and had a creamy-coloured sash around her waist. I didn't recognize the material, but it was breathtakingly beautiful. She had a shawl wrapped around her head and wisps of black hair were peeking out. She was standing very straight and her arms were by her side. Her face looked like a painting. Everything was perfect and beautiful. She must have been about seven feet tall, because she almost touched the ceiling.

I don't know how it happened because I didn't see her coming over to me, but the next thing I recall is being cradled in her arms like a little baby in the arms of its mother. A feeling of indescribable warmth and bliss came over me.

All too soon I could feel my body back in the bed and she was gone. I looked at my alarm clock and it was still 5.11 a.m. It had felt much longer than that. Sensing the importance of my experience, I grabbed a pen and wrote down everything I had seen and felt.

This experience has changed my perspective on everything. It wasn't a dream and it wasn't a hallucination – it really happened to me, I really saw an angel. I don't know why, as my life wasn't in danger that morning and I hadn't asked or prayed to see one, but I am so glad I did. It's changed me in so many ways. I'm still level-headed, practical and logical, but I'm willing to admit that it is often the things we can't predict or analyze, like love and compassion, that make the world a more rewarding place to live in. The only way I can describe it is that before my vision my life was in black and white, but now I see everything in all the colours of the rainbow.

Although their circumstances are vastly different, Joanna also found her life transformed when she saw an angel.

## A Calming and Beautiful Presence

I grew up very much the loner. My mum had seven of us to raise, so it was tough for all of us, but I think tougher for me because I didn't have the same dad as my brothers and sisters. I was also the youngest and soon after I was born my dad just couldn't handle Mum and her brood and left. I don't think she ever got over him leaving and didn't give me the love and nurturing every child needs. Life was hard and painful for me, but one encounter at the age of 14 changed all that. I will never forget it. I'm 67 now and it has stayed with me all my life.

One night I was wandering along some dark streets. I was really, really scared as the group of friends I hung out with had abandoned me and I didn't know where I was. I was terrified of being attacked. I must have been miles away from home. I had my bike with me but I couldn't really ride it as Mum had never got round to making sure I had lights.

I felt very vulnerable and this was rare, as life had taught me that the only way to survive was to be self-sufficient. But I was sweating with fear and sensed that if I didn't find my way home soon something bad would happen. I prayed for help and soon after I saw a bright light emerging from one of the dark sleepy houses on the street ahead. Out of this light came a young man. He had a calm and beautiful presence. He said he would help me and the next thing I can remember is waking up at home in my bed. I don't know how it happened and I shall never, ever forget it. What I do know is that when I think about that man I get a warm glowing feeling and it has helped me stay strong over the years.

A year or so later I left home and got my first job working in a factory. It was tough, but I had a new inner glow and I soon rose to supervisor and eventually to manager. Then I met a lovely guy and now I have five children of my own. My youngest, Paul, tells me he sees angels all the time. I don't doubt him because I have seen an angel too.

As mentioned previously, full-blown angel sightings like the ones shared with us by Joanna and the others in this chapter are incredibly rare. Angels are more likely to make their presence known in other ways. Some people hear angelic sounds beyond description. Others have a feeling of sudden warmth or comfort, or in times of sadness or grief they feel a gentle cloak of feathered wings wrapping softly around them. Sometimes there is the sudden rush of air created by the passing of an angel on a mission at the speed of light. This is often noticed at times of impending disaster. At other times, an inexplicable presence is felt. And sometimes, as was the case for Mary from Melbourne, Australia, there is no sensation at all, just a strong belief.

## A Miraculous Escape

Many years ago, when I was 18 years old, I obtained my driver's licence and, like any young person, I liked to drive a little faster than I should. One particular night I had just finished work and was on my way home. I was waiting for the lights to turn green at a very busy intersection and as soon as they changed, I put my foot down and drove full speed ahead.

What happened next is still a big puzzle to me today. All I remember is turning into a busy road, losing total control of the car and going across the opposite side of the road against all the oncoming traffic. At this point I shut my eyes tight, hoping that when I opened them again I would discover the whole thing had been a dream. But it wasn't. I was shocked to see a tram coming straight towards me.

Now this is where the miracle comes in, because I thought to myself, 'Oh my God, please help me.' The next thing I remember is opening my eyes and being amazed. My car had somehow managed to bypass all the traffic, totally missed the tram and ended up on the sidewalk on the opposite side of the road! The only thing that had stopped me from going through the brick wall was a 'NO STANDING' sign. My car didn't even have a scratch on it. Thank goodness there were no pedestrians walking by when my car went crashing through.

I can't believe I'm here telling you this story. It still puzzles me because by law my car should have been in a head-to-head collision with the tram and all the oncoming traffic. But I believe that my guardian angel saved me. I guess it just wasn't my time to go.

Claire also e-mailed to tell me about not one but two miraculous escapes. She put the first one down to sheer luck, but surviving the second accident has convinced her that her guardian angel is watching over her.

## Twice Lucky

I am 24 and over the last four years I have had two major accidents yet managed to walk away from both without a scratch.

The first happened when I went out for the day with my partner's mum and sister. Before getting into the car, my partner's sister asked if it would be OK if she sat in the middle seat instead of her usual place behind the passenger seat. I didn't see a problem with this.

Instead of taking the more usual route down the motorway we went down the country lanes. At one point I saw a dustbin lorry reversing. I was a bit hesitant about overtaking it, but my partner's mum told me to do so. We were all laughing and chatting, but then everything seemed to go quiet and the next thing I remember is my partner's mum screaming that there was a truck. It was too late and we'd been hit side on. The truck had been going over the speed limit and apparently our car span around three times!

When we came to a stop, it was pouring with rain. A man came to sit with us while we waited for the ambulance. He gave me his phone to call my partner and let us use his car for shelter. My partner's mum had a broken arm and fractured ribs and my partner's sister had whiplash injuries and her toenail had been ripped clean off.

The police report stated that if the passenger in the rear of the car had been sitting in the seat behind the passenger seat, it would have been more than likely that she would have been killed. It also stated that if my car had been going any slower or the truck had been going any faster, my car would have flipped over and we could all have been killed.

I walked away with no injuries at all.

My second major accident happened only a few weeks ago. I was driving to work at the airport and realized that I had forgotten my security pass. I turned around and headed back to the motorway. As I was coming round a bend, I felt as if someone else had hold of the steering wheel. My car pulled to the right and skimmed along the crash barrier and then all of a sudden it shot over to the left and moved over to the hard shoulder. Somehow it had managed to get from the fast lane to the hard shoulder without crashing into anyone else.

A couple who had been driving behind me had seen what had happened. They said first one tyre had blown out and then a second one had gone. They thought that I'd managed to steer the car really well and the fact that I'd not hit anyone else was amazing. The woman was called Anne. She and her husband sat with me for nearly an hour that day whilst the police took my details and moved my car. Yet again I walked away with no injuries.

My mum and I think that what happened in my first accident was just sheer luck. But the feeling I had on my second accident, and the fact that I walked away without a scratch again and also had Anne look after me, made me feel that I definitely had a guardian angel looking down on me.

Given the severity of both accidents, it's hard not to believe that a higher force was at work protecting Claire. Jackie certainly believes this to be the case for her. Here's her story:

## Angel Calling

About five weeks ago I was taking my 19-year-old son to his friend Laura's house for band practice. I dropped him off with his drum kit and then started to head home. Laura lives out in the sticks (a good thing really, as it's a heavy metal band) and her drive leads onto a country road. The road is very straight and narrow, only wide enough for one car, with small grass verges on either side.

It was very dark that night so I had my headlights on, but not full beam as I knew I would be able to see cars coming, as I was surrounded by open fields. The radio was on in the car, but not very loudly. I was going about 50 miles an hour when I heard a voice. It was not in my head or next to me, but was coming from the back of the car, over my left shoulder. Even now I can't say if it was male or female, but I know what it said: 'Mind you don't knock her over.' It scared me a little and I didn't dare look in my rear-view mirror for fear I would see somebody sitting there. Instead I concentrated on the road ahead.

Then, about 20 seconds later, I saw a woman walking towards me on the road with her dog. She was dressed in dark clothes, so could not be seen easily. I had to swerve up onto the bank to miss her. If I had not done so, I certainly would have hit her.

At the time I was really scared by the voice and I don't know how I managed to drive the few miles back to my home. Now I have had time to think about it and have read about other people's experiences, I feel differently and I am sure that it was an angel looking out for either me or the lady walking her dog or both of us. Either way, I certainly feel blessed that I had such an experience. I am a strong believer in life after death and I believe in angels, too, but in my wildest dreams I never imagined that I would have a message from an angel.

Mick, who believes that angels have helped him through many difficulties and sent me the bag lady story earlier, also sent me this one:

## One Boy and his Dog

In my job I spend a lot of time on the road driving between calls. Driving back from Worthing in West Sussex one day, I took a well-known short cut along 'B' roads that would save me some valuable time. As I started to accelerate away from a roundabout, I was forced to slow down: a boy was walking towards me with his dog on a lead. Although there was no pavement, there was ample grass verge for at the very least the dog to walk on. However, the boy continued to walk calmly towards me on the road with no attempt to divert his course.

Since a car was approaching from the other direction I was forced to slow down and let it past before pulling out almost to the other side of the road to avoid the child. Another car was approaching, but I had plenty of time to complete the manoeuvre. I looked at the boy as I passed, mentally asking, 'Why didn't you get out of the way?' As the other car drew close, I saw the driver lean forward in his seat and look up at me with a quizzical look on his face, which I interpreted as, 'Are you mad? What on Earth do you think you are up to?!' It was almost as if he hadn't seen the boy and his dog.

A little bemused, I accelerated hard along a straight bit of road before taking a long blind turn to the left. As I did so two cars approached me side by side, one overtaking the other. We probably had a closing speed of about 100 mph. I had enough time to reach the brake before the overtaking car, crammed with people, pulled in front of the other and averted disaster. I had a close-up view of a middle-aged lady's face and she was terrified. I have no doubt that we would have collided if it had not been for the boy and his dog slowing me down. Of course they could have been earthly creatures, but I believe they were angels sent to avert disaster.

Helen also wrote to tell me about her miraculous escape. She believes divine intervention saved her life.

## 'Move Over'

In 2002 I was driving to work along a major busy road in Adelaide. I was in the left-hand lane and had an Ute in front of me. The zone was 100kph, but I wasn't in any hurry so I was quite content to stay in the left lane and do 80. For some reason, though, I felt a bit agitated, as if something was telling me I needed to get over in the right-hand lane and do 100kph. But there was no option for me to pull into that lane easily, so I resigned myself to staying where I was.

Within seconds of deciding this, I saw a small gap that I could manoeuvre into and with one swift turn of the wheel, I changed lanes. Just as I did so, a very large piece of gyprock (inside-wall cladding) flew out of the Ute that had been in front of me and landed on the road where my car would have been, just missing the car that had been behind me.

I know someone was looking out for me that day. It's funny how even though I was quite patient and in no hurry, for some reason I kept feeling I needed to move over.

Clearly Helen listened to her inner angel – her intuition. Intuition also figures strongly in the next story, sent to me by Sally. Remember that 'nagging feeling' that mothers often get that we mentioned a few chapters ago? It figures powerfully in this story.

## 'Wake Up'

One morning I was playing with my baby daughter Lily on the living-room floor after a sleepless night. She was still waking four or five times. The doorbell rang and I went to get it. It was the delivery of a large bunch of flowers from some of the girls at work. I remember feeling touched but rather ungratefully also a bit put out, as I really didn't need something else to look after. I opened the baby gate that guarded the stairs and quickly nipped upstairs to place the flowers in the bathroom sink, ready to put in my bedroom later.

Then I went back to my daughter and after changing her I lay down with her on the floor and fell asleep. It was a deep and heavy sleep because I was so, so tired. I didn't dream, but after a while I heard a voice within me waking me up. It sounded as loud as a fire alarm. I woke up and my initial thought was that there was a burglar in the house. Then I looked for Lily. She wasn't in the room.

I ran to the front hall and saw immediately that I had forgotten to shut the stairgate. Then my heart stood still when I saw Lily balancing precariously at the top of the stairs. I grabbed her just before she fell.

It wasn't a dream, it wasn't a 'sense' that I should wake up, it was somebody who deliberately jolted me awake because my baby was seconds away from falling ten steps down onto a hard floor. I can't prove it, but I absolutely know it, and I am forever grateful to whoever and whatever it was.

Thank goodness Sally listened to her intuition here – which, I'll stress again, is so often the voice of our inner guardian angel.

With so many thoughts, feelings and sensations flying through our heads, I'm often asked how it is possible to know if it really is your inner angel speaking, or anxious fears and self-doubt. My answer is always the same: the voice of intuition is a lot gentler and calmer than the voice of fear. It always puts your best interests first and will build you up rather than pull you down. For example, if something isn't for you, your intuition won't tell you that you are stupid or a loser, it will nudge you gently in the right direction by telling you something doesn't feel right and encouraging you to move on and find what does work better for you. Also when you know something intuitively you know it without a lot of words to explain it, even if it seems illogical. When you are fearful, there are long drawn-out explanations that clatter around in your head – anything but a quiet knowing of the truth.

## Staying Young

We all have guardian angels who are willing to communicate with us, but most of the time we are just too busy and too 'grown up' in our thinking to listen to them. If, however, we are attentive and are willing to remain open to this communication, like the people whose stories are in this chapter, we can receive subtle messages from the angels within and around us that can enrich our daily lives beyond measure. In other words, angels can work with us only to the degree that we can hear them. Only when we can open ourselves up to growth can they lead us and help us feel young again, without the weight and burden of negativity, cynicism, resentment, fear, guilt and hate.

Angels are waiting for us to pause in wonder and to ask the way with the trust and faith of a child. Like the love a parent has for a child, the love your guardian angel has for you is unconditional. Your angel will stand by you even in the darkest hours of your life, helping you untangle seemingly impossible situations and supporting you through your worst fears, helping you discover the happiness and brilliance that is your birthright. You don't have to be perfect to be loved by your guardian angel, but you do need to have an open mind and trusting heart. And you don't have to be young in years to encounter an angel, but you do need to be young in heart and mind.

If you don't think angels are working in your life, perhaps you are not as receptive as you think. If angels find the doors to your heart and mind closed, they cannot enter. If, however, you can reconnect with the joy, passion and laughter of your inner child, the doors to your heart and mind will be flung wide open to let your angels in. Little miracles will begin to happen all around you. Angels will begin to speak to you through your heart and through everything and everyone, however ordinary.

If at this point in the book you are finding things a little hard to take on board, don't be hard on yourself. Take your time and come back later if you like. My aim is not to convince you that angels exist but to give you pause for thought. All the true stories in this book are from ordinary, honest and sincere people who believe that what they have experienced is real, and whether you believe them or not there is one fact that is undeniable: it simply isn't possible for us to see, hear or sense everything there is to know. Many things are beyond our understanding and nowhere is this illustrated more perfectly than in stories of healing angels – the subject of the next chapter.

Chapter 7

# Angels of Mercy

'The wisdom of the ages teaches that each
individual, whether believer or not, good or bad,
old or young, sick or well, rich or poor, has a
personal Guardian Angel with him or her at every
moment of life's journey.'

**Janice T. Connell**

Children are close to angels' hearts because they are
vulnerable and in need of protection, but as we've seen
there are also plenty of reports of guardian angels intervening in the lives of adults, particularly at times when
they, too, feel vulnerable, such as times of suffering or
illness. When we fall ill our minds and hearts may be
more receptive to angels because we tend to concentrate
less on the details that normally clog our thinking and
more on what and who really matters to us in life.

It seems that angels have the power to heal people,
both physically and emotionally. It's impossible to say

why they sometimes ease suffering and sometimes don't. All that can be said is that they know things about our spiritual development in this life and the next that are beyond our comprehension and we may never fully understand the reasons for them intervening in one case and not another. However, from the reports I have read and studied, there is no doubt in my mind that angels sometimes respond to situations or prayers or requests for help and their response makes a world of difference. Many of those who have been visited by an angel during times of physical or emotional suffering have their faith and attitude to life transformed as a result. Just knowing that their guardian angel is there when they need them strengthens their bodies and lifts their spirits.

Angels seem especially likely to help out when children are ill or suffering, but the stories in this chapter concern people of all ages, from babies to the elderly. What they have in common is the fact that each experience took place during a time of vulnerability or illness and provided the recipient with strength and support.

Each story also clearly demonstrates that however old or young, no one is beyond the love and protection of their guardian angel.

## Hospital Angels

Large numbers of healing angel experiences tend to occur in hospitals, which is no surprise really because a hospital is a place where people are sick and need help. The experiences can happen to the patients themselves or to relatives keeping vigil or to nurses and doctors and other hospital staff. I once interviewed a group of 15 nurses and eight of them told me they thought they had seen an angel at some point in the hospital. That's over half of them!

As we've seen in previous chapters, many women report angelic encounters when they are pregnant or giving birth. The maternity suite, however, isn't the only scene for angelic visitations. Angels can appear in any hospital ward.

In September 2008 Colleen Banton spoke to the press about her belief that an angel had saved her teenage daughter from certain death. The story was widely reported in the US media at the time, but for those of you who didn't catch it, here's a brief recap:

### Indisputably an Angel

Fourteen-year-old Chelsea had a history of serious health issues. She was born five weeks prematurely with developmental disabilities and had battled serious health problems all her life. She was particularly susceptible to pneumonia and in September 2008 she lay dying of it in a hospital room in Charlotte, NC.

Told that there was no hope for Chelsea, her mother Colleen instructed doctors to take her daughter off life support and allow nature to take its course. Then, as she watched her daughter fade away, an image of bright light appeared on a security monitor. Within an hour, Chelsea began a recovery that doctors are at a loss to explain. Colleen believes that the bright light was the image of an angel and that the apparition saved her daughter's life. 'It's a blessing,' she told NBC News. 'It's a miracle.'

Colleen took a picture of the image. Some who look at it would describe it as a flare of reflected light. Others – including nurses who were on duty at the time – say the three vertical shafts of light are indisputably an angel.

Colleen Banton's story is a dramatic and unique one because an image was captured photographically. More often than not when unexplained healing in a hospital setting, or anywhere else, takes place, there is no visual or documentary evidence, just personal testimony. To the person who has encountered an angel, however, belief in the reality of their experience is so strong that no 'proof' is required.

Rachel hasn't got a photograph or recording of her angelic healing experience, but there is no doubt whatsoever in her mind that an angel helped her. Here is a section of the e-mail she sent over to me:

## The Nurse in Green

I woke up at around 4.30 a.m. one morning with crippling abdominal pains. I had no idea what was wrong. I've normally got a very high pain threshold and am not one to pop a pill for a headache. So when I woke my husband and told him I was in agony, he knew something was wrong. I went downstairs and tried a drink of milk and some deep breathing, but nothing worked. In fact it was getting worse and spreading to my back. I couldn't keep still, it was that bad.

My husband insisted on calling an ambulance, which I thought was very silly. But then I looked in a mirror and saw I was turning grey. The paramedics arrived and said I really needed to go to hospital. I refused, as my husband was in the armed forces and was leaving at 10 a.m. to go on an exercise for a week, so there would be no one to watch our son. So with a shake of their heads the paramedics went, with the warning, 'These things don't sort themselves, Rachel.'

Around 10 minutes after they had left my husband rang his boss, who told him to stop being so silly and that his family was the most important thing, so I decided to drive myself to the hospital, which was around nine miles away.

I lied to my husband and said I was feeling better, but I was actually cold to the touch and sweating buckets, and I have no idea how I managed to drive myself to the hospital that morning. Thinking back, it was as if someone was controlling my hands and feet.

When I arrived, I went to reception. I knew they would have to take all my details, as I hadn't been there before, and that this would take about 10 minutes. I almost cried at the thought. I got to the desk and the lady asked for my name and date of birth. I gave it to her and she asked if I had been there before and I said I hadn't. She looked at me slightly oddly and said, 'Well, we have all your details here,' and it turned out that everything was already there, so I could go straight through.

I was taken to a cubicle and told to sit down, but I couldn't because it hurt too much, so I just kept pacing around. A nurse came back to take my blood and she left the line in my arm in case they needed more blood or to administer painkillers. After about 10 minutes a doctor came to see me and said, 'OK, 2mls is the most we can give you.' I looked at him and asked what he meant. He replied, 'Morphine, Rachel. We need to stop the pain.'

I was in so much pain, I agreed. But as the doctor was preparing the morphine I heard a lady's voice telling me that I didn't need it. So then I told the doctor I didn't want to take it. He looked at me and asked if I understood what I was saying. I said I did and that I was sure. Two more doctors and a nurse all came and advised me to have it, as it would work instantly, but I was determined. I signed a refusal form while writhing around in pain and I'm sure they all thought I was crazy.

I went and had an ultra-sound and X-rays, then came back to my cubicle. Suddenly I was overcome with exhaustion and lay down and instantly nodded off. I dreamed a sweet-faced nurse in a green uniform came into my cubicle and lifted up my T-shirt. She smiled at me and placed her hands on my stomach. When I asked her what she was doing, she just carried on smiling at me. Then she started massaging my stomach and it hurt. She said, 'Rachel, when you wake up you will feel fine.' I recognized her voice. It was the same voice that had told me I hadn't needed the morphine earlier.

Then I woke up and burst into tears. The pain had gone completely. I felt amazing. I looked down and my T-shirt was lifted up. I got up and looked for the nurse, but couldn't find her as all the nurses had blue uniforms.

The doctor came back and asked how I was and I said I felt perfect and asked to go home. He looked at me as if I was mad. He went on to tell me they suspected I had a severe kidney infection and they needed to keep me in on a drip. I told him I was fine, but he insisted that I wait for the blood test results. I sat there waiting with a smile and they came back all clear. The doctor said he had no idea why they were clear, but that I was free to go. I asked him where the nurse in the green uniform was, as I wanted to thank her, but he said that none of the nurses wore green. I was very confused.

I got out to my car, which had been parked up for seven hours in a clamping zone, but amazingly I hadn't been clamped. I drove home and my husband was waiting with a cup of tea.

I had been home for around 10 minutes when my husband asked if he could go on the exercise now, as I was feeling better. I was still feeling vulnerable, though, and didn't want him to go. I asked him what the chances of the exercise being cancelled were. When he heard that, he just looked at me and smiled, because I already knew the answer: they were *never* cancelled. I went upstairs to have a shower and a cry and while I was there I thought of my nurse and asked her to keep my husband there as I needed him. I felt it was pointless asking, but it did make me feel better.

We both fell asleep, exhausted, at about 7 a.m. At 9 a.m. we were woken by the phone ringing. It was my husband's boss. I sighed because I knew it would be the signal for him to join the exercise. He talked for a minute then put the phone down and smiled. The exercise had been cancelled. There was no reason for it, it just had. I thanked my lovely nurse in green.

Stories like Rachel's can't fail to warm the heart. She never saw the nurse in green with her waking eyes, but that nurse felt as true and as real to her as a member of her own family.

Amanda also believes she heard an angel call her name when she was in hospital. Here's her story:

## 'An Angel Called my Name'

I became extremely unwell quite suddenly with chest pains and difficulty breathing. It was a really large ovarian cyst which was pressing on my lung. I was taken into hospital, where I was given an emergency oophrectomy – the removal of the whole ovary – and had a partial removal of my Fallopian tube. Before the operation I told my fiancé that if he wanted to leave I would understand, as we didn't know if I would be able to have children after the operation. He absolutely refused and in fact became quite cross with me!

It was when I began to come around from the anaesthetic that I heard someone calling my name. I remember thinking it was the nurse, but she was sitting looking at the observation machine. Then I felt a weight on the other side of the bed and to my surprise saw my maternal granddad sitting there. He had actually died before I was born, but my brother, sisters and I were brought up with photos of him and stories about him. He looked as real as the nurse did, he had colour in his cheeks and I could feel his hand on mine. He told me not to worry about anything, the operation had gone well and everything would be OK. I felt calm and peaceful and as though he had been with me for the whole of my life. When I was wheeled out of the recovery room, my fiancé was waiting for me – he was the second angel I met that day.

Six weeks later, despite medical advice, I fell pregnant with my first child. The pregnancy wasn't easy. I had terrible pre-eclampsia and during the last months was hospitalized. Joshua's birth was hard and I was in labour for many hours. Finally I felt that I couldn't go on anymore. The midwife got the instruments ready, as she thought I was probably going to need help, and attached a probe to Joshua's head, as he was becoming distressed. My sister arrived with a packed lunch for my husband and he went and spoke to her while the midwife went to get some more things. Alone in the room, I shut my eyes. I felt so tired and just felt I couldn't go on. Then I heard someone say my name loudly and there was my granddad at the end of my bed. He said, 'I told you everything would be OK, now get on with it!' Joshua was born safely that very night with no intervention from the midwife.

Although my granddad didn't come to me in a blinding light with huge wings, he was my guardian angel and I feel a closeness to him that I cannot describe.

During times of suffering or poor health, angels draw closer to us than ever and this may explain the unusually high number of angel sightings in and around hospitals. Many of these accounts mention a bright or dazzling light similar to the one mentioned previously in the story about Colleen and her daughter Chelsea.

David explains what he experienced when he suffered from extreme food poisoning and spent two weeks in intensive care:

## A Light Experience

It was only afterwards that I realized how seriously ill I had been. At one point I was close to death. I don't remember much about the time when I was really ill, but I did have this one experience. I can't tell if I was asleep or not, but I remember feeling quite hot and throwing my left leg out from under the bedsheets. Suddenly, I felt warmth radiate from the bed and touch my leg. I lifted my head and saw a bright light shining on my leg. Then it gradually moved towards my chest and over my head. I had to cover my eyes, it was so strong. Then it was gone in a flash. I wasn't afraid, I only felt a deep sense of comfort and peace. I knew that I was out of danger and all would be well.

Kathy's story is similar, but varies in that the bright light appeared to take the form of a figure:

## The Figure Wrapped in Mist

When my son was about seven, he got German measles. The condition itself wasn't too serious but he developed an infection afterwards and became very ill indeed. He vomited every time he ate or drank anything and the fever was terrible – he burned to the touch. I got very scared and didn't know what to think when he told me that he could see things all around him and that they had faces.

He was taken to hospital and because his dehydration was so bad he was placed on a drip. That first night in hospital was the longest night of my life. The doctor let me stay over and I didn't sleep a wink at first. Eventually, though, at about 5 a.m., I fell asleep like a log. When I woke up, I had to shield my eyes because there was light all around my son. I couldn't move. At first I felt scared but then my fear subsided as the light started to resemble a figure, a figure wrapped in mist. Then it gradually melted away. I got up and ran to my son and saw that he was sleeping peacefully with a hint of a smile on his face.

He recovered gradually after that and within a few days he was allowed home. I didn't tell my husband about what I had seen because I knew he wouldn't believe me. I spoke to my son about it and he said he couldn't remember anything, but I'm still convinced I saw an angel of healing.

Sometimes healing angels manifest their closeness to patients not through lights or figures shrouded in light but through a feeling of comfort which Kim beautifully described in an e-mail to me as a 'cape of warmth':

## A Cape of Warmth

We lost my mom to cancer a year before my son Oliver was born. I had never felt her loss so badly as then and so wished that she was around to share him with us.

When Oliver was three months old, he had to have a hernia repair operation. It was a minor operation to everyone else, but I was worried sick. However, it all went to plan and he was in and out of theatre within an hour. I was so relieved when we went to fetch him back from the recovery room.

We stayed at the hospital for a further few hours to make sure he was fine and when the time came to leave, my partner went to fetch the car. I was just waiting with Oliver, who was in his pram, in a corridor when I felt what I can only describe as a huge 'cape of warmth' wrapped around my shoulders. It made me feel protected and safe and gave me the feeling that from now on Oliver would be fine and watched over. I'm sure that Mom was putting her arms around us both to give us a big warm hug to say that everything was OK now, which is exactly what she would have done had she been around. It was a truly amazing experience.

Kim's anxiety for the health and well-being of her child will strike a chord with loving parents everywhere. As a parent myself, I know that the most difficult pain to endure is that of one's children. Watching a child in distress or pain is a million times worse than enduring the pain oneself. It is particularly alarming when a child is rushed to hospital. Even though you know that hospital is the best place for that child to be, you also know how ill your child must be to be taken there. This is certainly how Sarah felt when she got a call from her 15-year-old son Connor's school saying he'd been taken to hospital with suspected meningitis.

## Extraordinarily Ordinary

That morning Connor hadn't been himself. He'd had the sniffles and seemed a bit irritable and tired. I'd wanted him to take the day off school, but he'd absolutely refused, saying that his football team needed him, as there was an after-school match. Knowing how much football meant to my son, I couldn't refuse.

I went to work. It was about 3 p.m. when the phone rang and the head mistress told me that I needed to get to the hospital as soon as possible. When I arrived I found

Connor in acute distress. He was hooked up to a penicillin drip and sweating profusely. He didn't seem to recognize me, but I squeezed his hand tightly and told him how much I loved him. He started to shout at me and became quite aggressive. It was terrifying. The doctor told me that this was the illness talking, not Connor. There was a lot of vomiting and when I felt Connor's head, it was scorching hot. I could tell how hard it was for him to breathe. Then he lapsed into a coma.

Faced with the very real possibility that my beloved son would die, I learned the meaning of fear that day. I watched helplessly as he was covered in monitors and attached to drips. I asked the doctor what his chances were of coming out of the coma with no physical or mental damage and he told me it was zero. The first night was a blur of tears and panic as I sat beside Connor watching and waiting. I'd seen this scene played out so many times in soap operas and movies. I couldn't believe that it was happening to me.

Just after midnight on the second night, I saw a figure dressed in white standing beside Connor's bed. At first I tried to ignore it, thinking it must be a hallucination brought on by my fatigue, but a few moments later a nurse came in to check on us and I noticed her staring at the same spot. I asked her if she could see an angel beside Connor's bed. She didn't reply directly, but told me that I shouldn't give up hope for Connor yet. I watched her check Connor and when she moved round to the side of the bed where the angel was standing she seemed to step around her. When she left the room the figure just melted away and within a split-second Connor started to regain consciousness. A day later he had fully emerged from his coma.

Connor spent a further two weeks in hospital and lost over two stone. The fact that he survived at all I'm convinced is down to the angel I saw that night. And I sense that the nurse saw something too, but for some reason didn't want to talk about it.

Shirley's story is interesting because it was her dreaming mind that took her to hospital:

## Bed Rest

About 25 years ago I was the young mother of two pre-school children and married to a sailor in the Royal Navy. My husband had recently told me that he had met some-one else and wanted to leave me and the children to be with her – not an unusual occurrence in naval circles, in my opinion.

Although I had half-expected this, it was still a terrible shock and I had no idea how I would manage without him. Looking back, I realize I sank into a deep depres-sion. I would somehow look after the children in the day, but nights would consist of long sleepless hours crying endlessly. With very few friends and no family nearby to help, I felt very alone.

I have always had an unshakeable belief in God and I spent many hours praying desperately for help. Help did indeed come one night when I was at my lowest ebb. I was sitting in bed when in my mind's eye I pictured myself in a hospital bed with two nurses on either side of me. They were talking together in such a way that I realized how overworked they were. They did not speak to me but continued with the banter and wrapped me in a warm blanket. I felt enveloped by an incredible warmth, love and peace, and with an overwhelming sense of gratitude, I fell into a much-needed sleep.

I woke the next morning with the knowledge that everything would be alright. In the weeks and months ahead, I was able to finally see my way out of my circumstances and change my life for the better.

I have often wondered why my angels appeared as they did, and I think that in some way it was specifically tailored for me. I will never cease to be grateful for their help at a time when I thought I was beyond help.

Shirley is spot on when she says she believes her experience was specifically tailored for her. Just as every person is unique, so every angel experience is unique to that person.

Of course, angels don't restrict their healing to hospitals. Pat's story is fascinating because she believes angels visited her before she even set foot in one:

## 'An Angel Saved my Life'

Once I had a really vivid dream that shocked me to the core. I dreamed I was being told by my doctor that I only had weeks to live because my bowel cancer had spread to the liver. It was horrible and I woke up really scared.

At first I tried to dismiss the dream as I was really busy working overseas and just didn't have time to go to the doctor, but when I returned home my secretary asked me if I wanted to do a company medical that year. I'd had one the previous year so would have declined, but my dream had frightened me and I thought I had better be safe than sorry. You probably know what happens next and you're right: the early stages of bowel cancer were detected. My doctor told me that if I'd waited any longer, or not had my medical that year, my chances of full recovery would not have been as strong.

I believe an angel sent me that dream and it saved my life. I was fully intending to skip my medical that year because it wasn't compulsory at my age and I was so busy. It was only because of the dream that I decided to have it.

Healing angels can also appear in the most unlikely places. Nathan's mother Sonia found hers in a swimming pool.

## Kissed by an Angel

When Nathan was born everybody said that he had been kissed by an angel because the groove above his lip was so deep. It made him look adorable. Anyway, fast-forwarding to his ninth birthday, I'd organized a private swimming party for him and five of his friends at the health club I worked at. It was one of the perks of the job being able to book the pool for an hour without anyone else there.

Everything was going great guns and then suddenly the boys started shouting to get my attention. Nathan had been practising his hand stands and had knocked his head. I leapt into the pool, dived under the water and pulled him to the surface. Then I dragged him to the side of the pool. I shouted to one of the boys to call 999 and tried to revive him. He was not responding and then I don't know what happened but I kind of froze in panic. I couldn't move. The boys were shouting at me and Nathan was just lying there in front of me. How I wished I had read my first aid manuals more closely. I didn't know what I should be doing and there were no swimming staff on hand to help out. I cursed myself for organizing the party and not thinking about safety.

And then a miracle happened: Nathan started to cough and a shower of water squirted onto my face. Soon he was up on his feet and wanting to get on with the party.

Later I asked him if he remembered anything between the time he hit his head and the time he woke up. He told me that he remembered me kissing him but there was another woman there kissing him as well and he didn't know who she was. She had to be his guardian angel, don't you think?

Tobias found healing angels on the internet:

## Soul Food

When I was a child my mum was always cooking and giving me sweet treats. I'd come home from school and cake and warm milk would be there. When I felt sad she'd give me chocolate to make me smile. Years later I was still eating chocolate in the hope that it would give me an emotional lift. Trouble was, I needed larger and larger quantities of food to feel comforted and safe. By the age of 37 my weight had ballooned to 25 stone. When my wife left me, I consoled myself by emptying the contents of my fridge. Food took away the pain. What I didn't realize was that it took away everything else as well.

The chest pains began when I was in my early forties. My doctor told me to lose weight and I said that I would give it a try. For a couple of weeks I went on a diet he gave me and felt wretched. Food was my comfort, my reward, my entertainment. Hopelessly addicted, I lived to eat, but no matter what I ate it was never enough.

The turning point came one night when I was watching some funny videos on YouTube. The familiar rumble of hunger in my stomach came and instantly I obeyed it by going to the fridge and taking out some leftover pizza. I went back to the computer and nearly dropped the pizza when instead of the video clip I had been watching I saw a video clip of myself. In the clip I was eating pizza and every time I took a bite I got thinner and thinner. I rubbed my eyes and when I opened them my image had gone and the video I had been watching was playing.

The experience freaked me out and I didn't sleep much that night. I tossed and turned, thinking about what I had seen. Instead of making me fatter, the food I was eating was actually making me disappear. And then it dawned on me – it wasn't nourishing me at all. What I needed didn't have any calories – because it wasn't food. It was emotional nourishment.

Until that experience the fact that I was using food to ease feelings of boredom, loneliness and anxiety had never really sunk in. But then I finally understood. Now whenever I feel hungry I think about what it is that I really need. I've got a long way to go, as I'm still over 20 stone, but I know I'll get there as I believe angels sent me that video clip. They knew how much I liked watching videos and realized it was probably the best way to reach me. And with angels on my side I can't possibly fail, can I?

Healing angels do crop up in all sorts of places. Christine met hers halfway up the stairs:

## Back Up Again

I had problems with my spine for four years and ME for 18 years. The first four years with ME, I was confined to my bed. One day I had improved a bit and had managed to go downstairs via our open-plan staircase, but on my way back up again, when I got to the last two stairs, I felt as if I was going to fall. I mentally cried out for help. Then I was aware of an amazing peace and love and saw two cherub angels hovering at my shoulders. They lifted me up by my shoulders and asked me to lean forward, as it would help. I made it up those last stairs with the help of angels.

Something similar happened to Ruby, who also walked away without an injury from a potentially fatal fall.

## Lifted Higher

I decided to go down to the basement to get a 40 lb bag of wood pellets for the stove, but halfway back up the basement steps, I started to fall. It was strange because I did feel a tiny bit scared but at the same time I had an amazing feeling of ease.

As I fell backwards the bag flew out of my hands and went falling way over to the left side of the steps. At that moment I felt myself being somehow jerked away from the steps, lifted higher and higher and then slowly, so slowly, lowered to the floor and my whole body put straight.

In Ruby's case, the angels didn't take a particular form, but sometimes, as this story reported in the newspapers in 2008 shows, healing angels can appear as babies.

## Baby Amelia

When 20-year-old Elizabeth Boyle collapsed in her Essex home, her 11-month-old daughter Amelia picked up a ringing phone. The baby repeatedly said, 'Mama' down the phone and raised the alarm to the caller, who was her grandmother, Linda Wright. Linda realized immediately something was wrong, as her daughter had a history of fainting and fitting, and dialled 999. Paramedics were dispatched to the scene. When they arrived, they found

Miss Boyle conscious but in a confused state. The mother was later told how her phone had been answered by her daughter and how the baby had played such a vital role in getting help.

There is really no limit to the ways in which angels can reveal themselves to us. Rachel's letter below is fairly typical of many I have received from people who believe that they also leave signs of their healing presence.

## A White Rose

I was going through a particularly hard time in my life. I was confused as to where I was going and on the verge of splitting up with the love of my life due to the frustrations of our life, the main ones being no money or jobs. My partner was waiting on an answer from the armed forces regarding rejoining and we were so tight with money that some days we didn't eat so that our two-year-old son could.

One day, after we had just had a huge argument, I walked out of the house in tears. I had no money for a bus or taxi and started walking and walking. I must have walked for around seven miles into town, not really noticing how long I had been out or the fact that it was raining. I ended up in a big cemetery close to the town centre. I have always found cemeteries calming and relaxing.

I walked through the old part of the grounds with my head down. When I looked up I saw a bench and sat and cried and cried from the depths of my soul. I looked up to the sky and said aloud, 'Why can't anyone help us? Why is this happening to us? Please anyone.' I had no idea who I was talking to or why I was speaking out loud.

After sobbing for a while longer I got calmer and decided to head back home. I had no phone with me and people would be getting worried. I started walking back the way I had come and had only taken a few steps when I saw in the middle of the path, right where I had walked before, the head of a white rose. It was perfect. There was not a mark on it, even though it was on the wet floor. It was the most brilliant white I had ever seen. I looked at the graves nearby for the flowers but they all dated back to the 1600s and had no flowers on them. It couldn't have been there earlier as I would have walked over it on the narrow path. I had no idea how it had got there but it took my breath away. I felt instantly calm, thanked whoever had given me the rose and started on the long walk home.

It was dark and cold. I had no coat and it was still raining hard. I had walked for about a mile when I saw a phone box that was lit up brightly. I went inside to shelter for a minute, hoping the rain would pass. I turned to look at the phone and had the urge to check inside the change slot. Right there was enough money for the bus and for me to call my partner at home, who was sick with worry as I had been gone for hours.

I stepped out of the phone box and as I did so my bus turned up. I went home with a smile on the inside and the outside – and you know what, the next day my lovely partner got his call from the army and he was in.

Rachel went on to tell me about another angelic experience she had when her best friend Anthea took her own life.

## Butterflies

When my best friend Anthea died I was carrying my daughter. Anthea was going to be her godmother. One of my favourite memories of her was that she had a hairclip that looked like a butterfly and in her ebony hair it looked beautiful. During the funeral we went outside to look at the flowers and despite it being December I saw the two most beautiful butterflies flying around them. I couldn't believe I was seeing them and it made the coming months so much easier to deal with.

As my daughter Millie grew older I hoped that Anthea was watching over her and her brother Josh. The time that really stands out, though, is when Josh was in reception at school and was having a hard time and not settling easily. As I left him one day I prayed to Anthea to watch over him for me. When I picked him up, he came out positively glowing and told me the butterfly lady had come to see him when he was in the bathroom and told him to be strong and that she would look out for him. I pressed him for more information, but all he would say was the butterfly was in her hair. He had only been two when Anthea passed away. I am convinced to this day that it was her.

The last time I 'saw' Anthea was when I dreamed of her standing in a beautiful garden dressed all in purple. All around her and on her hands were butterflies. She didn't speak, but I sensed her peace and when I woke up I had mine too.

My angels aren't what you would normally expect and I accept that I saw them when I was going through a hard time and when I was heavy with grief, but I believe wholeheartedly that what I saw and felt was real.

Although Rachel senses the healing presence of angels through signs and dreams, it seems that her young son Josh has the ability to actually see his guardian angel.

As this story sent to me by Sharon illustrates perfectly, angels can also manifest through our heartfelt prayers:

## 'Listen to Me'

I am a mental health nurse and have been visiting a man with terminal cancer to offer him emotional and psychological support. During my initial visits he was really struggling and was exhibiting involuntary body movements. His head would jerk back and his body would shake uncontrollably and this made it difficult for him to hold a conversation with me. I offered him relaxation techniques, which his wife was happy to facilitate, and these did help a little, but only gave him short periods of relief.

I continued to visit him every two weeks and his involuntary body movements also continued. Talking made him anxious and his wife almost always had to speak on his behalf. I felt medication would help, but he was adamant that he would not consider it, as he had had a bad experience with medication in the past.

I was feeling concerned that I was not helping him enough. After one visit, I was emotional and close to tears. Driving to my next appointment, I banged the steering wheel in frustration and declared out loud, 'Please God, why won't he just take medication? Why should he have to suffer like this?'

The next visit came round and I rang the doorbell as usual, wondering how the last two weeks had been for him. To my surprise, I was greeted not by his wife but by the man himself, minus the shakes and jerks. He was completely still and composed. I was lost for words. Tears filled my eyes once again, but this time tears of joy.

As we sat in his front room he explained that he had gone to the doctor some days after our last conversation and been prescribed some medication to help relax his muscles. He had been taking it and had been without the shakes and ticks for over a week. I expressed my joy and thanked him for considering my recommendations.

I am still visiting every fortnight and he is now driving his car on short journeys and is enjoying a more active life. He still lives with terminal cancer but that is not getting any worse. His oncologist is pleased and I am delighted.

Now I know that it is the medication that is giving him the quality of life, but that day I asked for help for him I believe angels intervened and made him see sense. One day I actually asked them for proof and funnily enough during a conversation later on his wife told me her maiden name was 'Angel'. Now that's surely not a coincidence?

We are reading this story from Sharon's perspective, but it's fascinating to consider that if we were reading it from her patient's perspective, he might regard *her* as an angel because her passionate concern for his well-being prompted him to take the best course of action. And perhaps she was. Perhaps in the right time and place we can all be healing angels. Perhaps, like Sharon, we can all be instruments of the extraordinary, offering compassion and simple kindness that can help others feel that they have been touched by an angel.

## Angel Animals

This chapter and indeed this book just wouldn't feel complete without mention of a unique and very special group of healing angels – animals. Just as children can teach us spiritual lessons about being spontaneous, passionate and open to the wonder all around and within us, animals have much to teach us about patience, trust, compassion, healing and love.

As ever, it seems that children share a special closeness with them. It's not surprising really when you consider that both animals and children are naturally intuitive and therefore more open to the divine interconnectedness of all things.

There have been some remarkable stories in the press in recent years highlighting the special affinity between animals and angels, and here is just a brief snapshot of them:

A seven-year-old Indian boy allegedly survived the Boxing Day tsunami when his dog 'nipped and nudged' him up a hill to safety.

In 1996 a gorilla at Brookfield Zoo, Chicago, picked up and cuddled a three year old who had fallen into its enclosure, then returned the child to zookeepers.

In 1986 five-year-old Levan Merritt was cradled by a gorilla at Jersey Zoo after falling 20ft into its enclosure.

In 1998 police trying to rescue a 'feral' boy near Moscow were held off by the dogs who had become his friends.

Chimpanzees are said to have looked after a two-year-old disabled boy for a year when he was abandoned by his nomadic tribe in Nigeria in 1996.

These stories are incredible without doubt, but just as awe-inspiring to my mind is the love, compassion, devotion and companionship that animals and pets give not just to children but to their loving owners every day of every year. So many people have told me they believe animals have a soulful connection to a higher force, uniting all of us in an unconditional bond of love. Here are just a few of the comments:

## 'Angels in Fur'

My current cat is truly a loving, wonderful, 'heaven sent' companion and is certainly as far as I am concerned a real living angel. She senses my grief and turmoil and just instinctively knows when to come and curl up with me.

**Mike**

I've thought for a long time now that my pets are earth-bound angels sent here to encourage us and teach us. I truly believe that animals are angels in fur. My dogs and cat bring out the qualities in me that I like best and time spent with them is a gift.

**Caitlin**

I owe my life to my dog Samson. I got him a year before my husband died and without him there beside me I would have been sucked up by grief. He is like a father and mother, brother and sister and friend to me. I love him beyond belief.

**Laura**

They may not be angels in the traditional sense, but with their empathy, devotion and unconditional love, animals sound a lot like angels to me. Like angels, they simply love us and watch over us in this life and the next. I couldn't think of a better place to put this enchanting story sent to me by Andy:

## All about Poe

Everyone thinks that their pets are special. That's why we love them so much. But Poe really was an extraordinary cat. He was more like a little puppy than a cat. He would scamper about and he was into everything. My other cats, Pepsi, Parsley and Jewel, are hostile when an intruding cat dares to cross the garden, but Poe would run up to the stranger, head held high, and touch noses with it, keen to make friends. He had a verve and a zest for life that were wonderful to watch. He didn't have a negative patch of fur on him. That's why it was so heartbreaking when he died in my arms after being hit by a car at the young age of 18 months.

I was totally devastated. I didn't know if I could go on without my furry boy. I cried and cried, never wishing to dry my tears. Then, three days after I'd lost him, I was sitting in the conservatory when I suddenly got such an overwhelming sense of Poe's presence that I smiled for the first time in those three days. The sensation was sharp and sudden and I instantly realized that Poe hadn't gone anywhere – he was still right there with me.

I felt compelled to get up and go into the garden and that's when it really hit me! The force was such that I had to catch my breath and take a step backwards. 'This is where he is,' I thought. 'He's in the garden and the woods beyond. He's part of nature now.' I knew beyond doubt that my darling Poe was right by my side and would be forever more.

I hadn't read anything like it before, but your book *An Angel Called My Name* jumped off the shelf at me. I began to read it and realized that Poe was an angel watching over me, calling my name whenever he thought I needed him. Then something strange happened. I was reading the chapter that explained how angels often showed their presence by the appearance of a white feather. I put the book down, thinking that this was becoming a little far-fetched, when a white feather drifted down out of a clear blue May sky and landed right at my feet. I looked up and said, 'Oh, thank you, Poe. Just when I was doubting, you sent me a sign.'

This was the start of an intense period of coincidences, synchronicities and visitations that happened almost daily. Space precludes me from listing them all, but they were so striking and abundant as to be way beyond chance and probability. I actually got a bit frightened at one point, because it was clear that I was in the midst of something supernatural and I didn't know where it was going. But the mysterious events were accompanied by extremely strong feelings of Poe's presence reassuring and calming me.

In the tragic aftermath of losing Poe, I had vowed to do two things in his memory: set up a memorial pen in his name at an animal rescue centre and get a voluntary

Saturday job helping animals at such a centre. It took much longer than I anticipated to arrange these two things and at times I felt like giving up. But on these days of doubt (and on no other) I would see white feathers in prominent places. This was undoubtedly Poe telling me not to give up.

One day in September I planted some bluebell bulbs around the memorial tree that I had planted in the woods that Poe so loved to explore. I had just finished this labour of love when I got a call from Preston RSPCA to tell me that the plaque was in place on Poe's memorial cat pen. I went over to see it and was stunned to see a young black cat, the absolute image of Poe, was the first cat in the pen. And his name was Bluebell! It's also worth noting that to get to Preston RSPCA from my house, you go down a road called Bluebell Way. These are the kind of things that were happening that simply could not be mere coincidence.

Shortly afterwards I had my volunteer application accepted at Preston RSPCA. I walked through the woods, mentally thanking Poe for encouraging me. I came back home and my mouth fell open at the sight of a white feather right in the middle of my living-room floor!

With this, the intense period of mysterious occurrences ended. Perhaps I had come to realize that Poe was at peace so I was able to summon the courage to let him go. He still pops in to say hello, though, and at times of doubt and upheaval he shows me the way.

For my volunteering, I was torn between two rescue centres, but Poe was sending me clear signs that he wanted me to work at the RSPCA. At the time I didn't know why. I do now! I recently took voluntary redundancy from my mundane soul-destroying job and have been lucky enough to get a position as an animal care assistant at the RSPCA, my absolute dream job. I'm convinced that Poe knew that all this was going to happen and he was guiding me towards it.

One nice little footnote: I adopted a particularly needy little kitten and called her Bluebell, in tribute to the first young cat to be housed in Poe's memorial pen. At first she couldn't get the hang of the catflap at all. For five long days I tried to teach her how to use it but just had a bemused feline looking back at me. Finally, in desperation I said out loud, 'Poe, if you're here, can you show her what to do?' Bluebell instantly cocked her head to one side, listened intently, then pushed straight through the catflap. She has never had a problem with it since. I was overjoyed because I felt this was indisputable proof that Poe approved of me getting Bluebell and was watching over her.

Thank you, Andy and Poe, from the bottom of my heart, as I know this story will resonate with people who have loved and lost pets everywhere!

In his story Andy mentions coincidences as one of the ways in which angels speak to us. I wholeheartedly agree and there's more about this special angel calling card in the final chapter. Andy also talks about his firm belief that Poe is watching over him, a phenomenon so often reported by owners who have lost their beloved pets that it is impossible not to take it seriously. Here's an e-mail from Pam:

## Fudge

A few years ago my husband and I adopted a rescue dog from our local RSPCA. He was about 11–12 years old and had led the most awful life imaginable till then, being just one of almost 300 dogs kept in one house. Kept in cages piled on top of one another, fed on slops, rancid green water – I guess you have the picture. Over the next few months he began to trust us and we loved him more with each passing day. We called him Fudge.

About four weeks ago we started to find the odd feather about the house, just small white ones. At the time we thought nothing of it. Living in the country, where birds are often a cat's dinner, there seemed nothing strange in that.

Sad to say, 10 days ago we had to say goodbye to our Fudge. It was by far the hardest thing we have ever had to do, but as he was 18 years of age, almost blind, deaf, very arthritic and had a failing heart, it was kinder to say goodbye than to see him struggle to stay with us.

Last Monday, after doing some spring cleaning, I happened to mention that we had seen no more feathers since Fudge's passing. After we had eaten our evening meal and I had caught up with a few things on the PC, I left the office and there it was, on the floor where Fudge used to lie: the most beautiful pure white feather. I truly believe that it was a sign from Fudge to let us know he was happy and heaven had another beautiful angel. The feathers we found prior to his passing I firmly believe were from his guardian angel just paving the way for him. I have taken great comfort from finding the feather. I know now that we did the right thing by him, hard though it was. He has let us know that.

The stories so far have focused only on dogs and cats, but wild animals, birds and even insects can walk beside us as angels if we open our hearts and minds to them. Sharon e-mailed this rather unusual angel story:

## The Red Admiral

I got married in early December. I had always wanted a winter wedding. At the evening reception, as my husband and I stood waiting for our guests, something caught my eye, and when I looked more closely there was a red admiral butterfly on my shoulder. I was astonished, as it was December and pretty cold! As the guests came in I warned them to be careful not to squash my little friend as they hugged me. After a while I became worried that this would happen anyway and almost on cue it flew off and landed on the wall above the table my parents were sitting at. I looked up occasionally to check and it didn't move from its perch all night.

I later learned that butterflies symbolize a new beginning. I imagine that one must have been sent to wish me well on my big day and in my new life. I have a photograph of it and look at it if I feel down or alone, as it reminds me that someone is looking out for me.

Sue kindly sent me this story which once again shows that animal angels love us and watch over us in this life and the next:

## Timmy and Marvine

A couple of weeks ago we lost two out of three budgies in a week: Timmy, a violet-coloured bird, and Marvine, a grey one. We thankfully still have Paddy and had recently given a loving home to two cockatiels. I'm convinced they came into our lives just before we lost our two budgies to help ease the pain.

When he wasn't well, we took Timmy to an avian vet. He was kept in for tests and sadly he never came home again. Later that week Marvine didn't seem right and we made an appointment at the vet's for her for the next day, but during the evening I took her out and cuddled her and I just knew she wouldn't get to the vet. I said, 'Please, dear angels, if you are going to take her to join Timmy, please make it soon so she will not suffer.' The angels must have been listening, as when we came down the next morning we found she had passed over.

The next day we were going shopping in the car and as I got in I saw a feather of Marvine's on the back seat. It hadn't been there before and I was so glad to have it for a keepsake.

The next morning as we were having breakfast, I became aware of a bright patch on the wall behind me. It was pouring with rain at the time, so it could not have been sunlight. I asked my husband if he could see it and he said he couldn't see anything. It only lasted a few seconds before it faded.

The following day I was doing some housework and I realized I didn't have a feather of Timmy's. Then something told me to look behind the sofa. I pulled it out and there, caught in the fabric at the back, was one of his feathers.

Timmy and Marvine were very much a part of our family and I sense they haven't left us. I'm sure they will visit us from time to time and will let us know they are well and happy in their new home.

I could write so much more about animals doing the work of angels and helping to keep us young in heart and close to spirit, but space and time don't permit it here. Perhaps that will keep for another book, but just before we move on to the next chapter I'd like to finish up with a story about another angel in fur called Sam.

## Sam the Koala

In early 2009 a bewildered and badly burned koala emerged from the ashes of Australia's deadliest bushfires and went on to become a beacon of hope after days of devastation and the loss of more than 180 lives.

Volunteer firefighter Dave Tree came across the stricken koala, affectionately named Sam, cowering in a burned-out section of a forest at Mirboo North, some 150km southeast of Melbourne. As a colleague filmed him, he approached the koala and offered the terrified animal some water, gently talking to it until it put a paw on his hand and began drinking from the plastic water bottle.

'Things do survive the bushfire. There's a koala here. You alright, buddy?' said Mr Tree in the video which was posted on the video-sharing website YouTube. The koala, which turned out to be female, was taken to the Southern Ash Wildlife Shelter in Rawson, while her photos, taken on a mobile phone, spread quickly across the globe.

The story was reminiscent of that of another koala, named Lucky, who survived the bushfires that destroyed about 500 homes with the loss of four lives in the Australian capital of Canberra in 2003. Lucky became a symbol of hope as people rebuilt lives after the fires and was cared for in a nature reserve.

Chapter 8

# Angels in Waiting

'Heaven comes to people – and their loved ones –
when they are dying. It is not uncommon for
angels to appear when people are on the edge of
death, and people who have had near-death
experiences often describe feelings of
indescribable peace and angels.'

**Gary Kinnaman**

We are never more childlike, vulnerable and in need of comfort and healing than when a loved one dies or when we ourselves are on the edge of death. Nothing concentrates or unhinges the mind more than the shadow of death. Faced with it, people who have never believed in angels may find themselves wondering if there's a heaven and if they or their loved ones will live on in an afterlife. And at the opposite end of the spectrum people who have always believed in a heaven may begin to have doubts when death, that great unknown, snatches a child or someone in the prime of life. But what causes adults to become distraught and frantic is quite natural to children.

## Children Don't Believe in Death – They Know Better

In fact the very words 'children' and 'heaven' seem to fit together. I have received letters and reports from all over the world which state that prior to death children have talked about heaven and seen angels watching and waiting for them to cross over. Whether dying themselves or witnessing or hearing about the imminent death of someone else, many children have comforted adults and taught them that death simply does not exist.

As we've seen throughout this book, children are close to the world of spirit because they have not built up an inhibiting wall of fears and opinions. Sometimes they can even tell adults what it looks like. It may be hard to make sense of this at first, but in the great majority of cases they talk with eager anticipation about going into a world of light which is much more beautiful than this one. They talk of extraordinary things, such as singing flowers and dancing rainbows, and being surrounded by angels who love and take care of them.

One six-year-old boy I talked to showed a clear awareness that the grave is not the place where those who have died end up. I asked him if he had been to visit his grandfather's grave to lay some flowers on it and he told me quite sharply that there was no point because only a bit of his grandfather was in the grave and the rest of him was 'hovering' around. I asked him what he meant and, rolling his eyes as if bored by my stupidity, he told me that his grandfather's body was in the ground but the rest of him was very much alive and watching over him.

A year previously, when his grandfather had still been alive but dying of cancer, the boy had told his mother that he could see angels around him. He also said he saw his grandfather's body of light, which was healthy and happy. His words were a great comfort to his mother and helped her cope better with her father's death.

Eight-year-old Lara also reassured her parents in the months prior to her death from degenerative heart disease. She would often talk about the visions she had of heaven and the afterlife. Her mother Monica kindly sent me a recording of her daughter speaking the month before she died and I've transcribed a section of it for you here:

I like it in heaven. There is only sunshine and music and colour. Tiny angels play with me. I have a face but I don't know what I look like and everywhere there are waves of light. I have a body too but I don't know what it looks like. The buildings are made of light too. You can see and feel them, but they are not there. There is no time, because it is faster than time. I never get bored there. Everything that you can get is of the best. Here on Earth it is also fine, but we just don't know any better. My real home is there.

There is almost a sense from reading Lara's thoughts that even when she was alive she was already living in heaven. Her words make me think of a poem written by Hans Christian Andersen and published in 1827:

## A Dying Child

Mother, I'm so tired, I want to sleep now;
let me fall asleep and feel you near.
Please don't cry – there now, you'll promise, won't you?
On my face I felt your burning tear.
Here's so cold and winds outside are frightening,
but in dreams – ah, that's what I like best;
I can see the darling angel children
when I shut my sleepy eyes to rest.
Mother, look, the angel's here beside me!
Listen, too, how sweet the music grows.
See, his wings are both white and lovely;
surely it was God who gave him those.
Green and red and yellow floating round me,
they are flowers the angel came to spread.
Shall I, too, have wings while I'm alive, or—

Mother, is it only when I'm dead?
Why do you take hold of me so tightly,
put your cheek to mine the way you do?
And your cheek is wet, but yet it's burning – Mother
I shall always be with you …
Yes, but then you mustn't go on sighing;
when you cry I cry as well, you see.
I'm so tired – my eyes they want to stay open –
Mother – look – the Angel's kissing me.

This poem is called 'A Dying Child', but don't you think it should be retitled 'A Living Child'?

Here's a breathtaking story sent to me by Michael, who 'died' at the age of seven. In his deathbed vision he encountered Jesus but, as discussed before, angels are attached to no particular religion, creed or belief system. The only language they speak is a universal one of love, though sometimes they choose to manifest this love through images and experiences that speak to the belief system and therefore the heart of the individual experiencing them.

## 'The Day I Died and Went to Heaven'

I was lying in my bed in a single room in Middlesbrough General Hospital in the May of 1956. I was paralyzed all over, apart from the area closest to my heart. The consultant had made my mother aware that I only had about three hours to live. She had first met him when she had been nursing at Derby and he had been a junior doctor, so he had realized that she knew about the illness and therefore the truth had to be told.

That evening, when visiting time was over, she went home. In those days there was only a short time for people to visit. I cannot imagine how she felt.

Afterwards I was feeling very peaceful, although a little sad because my mother had gone. Then suddenly I was aware that I was no longer in my hospital bed but standing up, and there in front of me, sitting on a wooden table, was Jesus. On my right stood my maternal grandfather, who had died 15 years before I was born. The room was brilliant white and Jesus was dressed all in white with a sash of purple, red and white with gold thread running through the red. To his left were the most magnificent angels you could ever imagine. I believe there were about four or five of them. On the table was a brown paper parcel and I heard Jesus say to the angels that the parcel contained my life and he would like them to take it to my hospital bedside so that I would live.

I have a vague memory of seeing more of the world of spirit or heaven, but I cannot say what, or if I was told why I had to return to Earth or what my future was going to be. I was also not aware of any nurses checking on me at this time. I do know that when I woke up in my hospital bed I was no longer paralyzed from the waist up. Later I would learn to walk.

The experience had a profound influence on Michael, who went on to practise healing himself as a registered mental nurse.

It's not just children, of course, who see angelic visions around death. People of all ages have reported this phenomenon. It seems that death makes children of us all.

## Watching and Waiting

Many people who have written to me have reported seeing an angel waiting beside the bedside of a dying person before they passed away. When Joan's brother was dying she remembers coming into his bedroom and seeing an angel standing at the foot of his bed. 'The angel was fairly small,' she said, 'but its wings were enormous and seemed to be wrapping themselves around my brother.' Sometimes there is no figure, just a glowing light. These visions can arise weeks or even months before the death or just moments before the person slips away, but they are always a source of incredible comfort.

I'm sure you'll be moved by this very short story sent to me eight years ago now by a man called Thomas:

## The Day after Tomorrow

On 10 January 1951 my five-year-old daughter died. Before she went, she told me that she could see angels at the foot of her bed. She waved to them and said she would see them the day after tomorrow. She died 48 hours later.

Jean, too, saw an angel when her grandmother died:

## An Angel Then and Now

From an early age my mother had always told me that an angel would be there when I needed one. She told me she had been visited by one when she was close to death. Her baby had been stillborn and she had lost a lot of blood. She knew she was very ill and her family had been told that she was unlikely to survive. She told me how when she was at her lowest a beautiful nurse in white sat with her, held her hand and spoke calmly to her, leaving her with peace and a newfound strength. When she recovered she asked about that nurse and tried to find her, but no one knew her. Then Mum knew it had been an angel.

As I grew older I didn't think much about angels. I was too busy. My grandmother lived with us and I loved her probably more than anyone else. She always had time for me. When she was 88 she suffered a series of small strokes and I was devastated. I was just 12 and couldn't imagine that anything could happen to her. Then she had a massive heart attack and was rushed to hospital. When Mum and Dad came back they tried to prepare me for the worst, as Gran was unconscious, but I didn't want to know.

I went into Gran's empty room. It was dark, but the curtains were open. I think I was crying. I was aware of a bright light outside the window and I looked out. A boy of about 16 with blond curly hair and a white shirt was standing on the windowsill. He smiled at me and I am sure he said, 'Don't worry, I will find her in time.' I suddenly felt calm and shouted for my mum to come and see, but when I turned around he was gone. I told my mother, but before she had the chance to ask me anymore about it the phone rang to say that Gran had died. Surprisingly, I wasn't as upset as I thought I would be. I knew everything was alright.

Weeks later, when Mum and I were going through Gran's things, we found some photographs. I got very excited, as one of them was a picture of the boy on the windowsill. Mum explained that it was her brother, who had died when he was 16, some 30 years earlier. When I said it was the boy I had seen, she smiled and said, 'He was an angel then and is now, and had come to find his mother.'

It's been 40 years now since that experience and although I have never seen an angel since I am very aware of being looked after by them and believe strongly that through love all in this world and the next can be united.

## Near-Death Experiences

Every day people are pulled back from death thanks to advances in science and medicine, but just as – if not more – miraculous is the fact that a staggering 40 per cent of them claim to have had an experience of another reality that exists beyond death. There is much debate today about these experiences – known as near-death experiences or NDEs – with experts arguing that they can be explained physiologically, for example by oxygen starvation to the brain or as a result of various drugs being taken. What none of these arguments really takes into account, however, is the startling fact that there is typically a strong degree of similarity between these experiences – light, tunnels, passages, joyful faces, etc. – and that they have a profound and very positive impact on the lives of those who have undergone them.

Louise wrote:

I was very ill in hospital and I think everyone had just about given up hope for me. I started to float towards a tunnel. It was dark until I went into it and then it lit up. It was gone in a flash, but I will never forget it.

Another lady who e-mailed me had been diagnosed with cancer and was undergoing surgery:

## Counting Down

I remember counting down from ten after I'd been given my injection and then I had this most amazing vision. I was floating backwards through a passage with my head travelling towards a source of light and my feet towards the operating theatre. As I floated, I turned around and saw beneath me rows of happy smiling faces, all pointing at me with excitement. I felt like a star arriving on the red carpet – only there was only brilliant white all around me. I believe I saw heaven. The next thing I remember is waking up with a dry mouth and a sore throat in the recovery room.

Clara nearly passed over immediately after giving birth. Here is her story:

## Fading Away

I have numerous angel stories, but one of the most uplifting happened when I had delivered my second child. All was going well and we were waiting for the placenta to come out, but after an hour there was still nothing. The doctors gave me an injection and then it came out and I felt blood pouring from me. I asked them to take the baby, as I was fading away. They told me not to be daft, but then I blacked out.

The next thing I was somewhere else. I say now it was a room but think that is my head trying to fit what I saw into an image I understand, as I more felt things than saw them. In this 'room' I was with two women. One was my nan, who had ten children and was the one person I looked up to and wanted to be like when I was younger, without realizing it at the time. My head never warmed to her but I now know my heart did. The second was my great granddad's sister Clara, after whom I am named. She was around a lot when I was growing up.

I was surrounded by the most intense feeling of love you could ever imagine and I finally felt as though I belonged, as though I was home at last. I was so happy to be there and my life on Earth wasn't even in my mind, but my nan and Clara spoke to me and said it wasn't my time. I had to go back, as I was going to have an exceptional child. I argued I didn't want to go back. They told me I had to and all of a sudden everything went black and I felt as though I was being dragged back. I felt sick to my stomach. Then I opened my eyes and saw my husband holding an oxygen mask over my face and instantly the bad feeling went. I am so glad it was him holding the mask, as it made returning to my body much easier to take.

My mother had terminal cancer at the time and she sadly died just over a year later, before my third daughter was born. I was with her when she passed over. I was sad but also jealous of the fact that she was going home to all that love.

## Sad and Happy

Clara also sent in this sad but happy story about pregnancy, birth, loss and love. It made me cry and smile at the same time when I read it.

## Two Little Boys

I have four daughters and when I had my fifth child I was totally stunned to hear them say the words I never thought I'd hear: 'It's a boy.' My friend was pregnant too and due the day after me. But sadly when she had her 20-week scan it was found that her son only had half a heart. He had only a 1/12,000 chance of surviving pregnancy and with half a heart would not survive once he was born.

When I talked to her about it, a song kept going through my mind, 'Two Little Boys', a song about two brothers who grow up together to fight in the American civil war. I also kept hearing the crying of a baby. It hardly felt appropriate under the circumstances, but the crying and the song were so insistent in my head that I had to tell my friend about them. I told her that there was room in my heart for two boys, so to please share mine with me and be his godmother. She told me that the song 'Two Little Boys' meant a lot to her and if she was ever sad or ill her mum would sing it to her, so it was a song that brought her great comfort.

She is my son's godmother now and firmly believes her son is my son's guardian angel and that they play together. As for the crying in my head, it stopped as soon as my friend made the decision to let her son go. I took this to mean that he was in pain or unhappy before, but he wasn't once she had let him go back home.

Sometimes it does appear that death has a healing and bonding effect on people – however far apart life may have taken them. Charlotte sent me the following story:

## Stopwatch

My husband worked in an office all day and one day some of the girls there asked him to help with their jogging training. I told him he should get fit first and lose some weight, as it was dangerous to jog with too much weight.

Our marriage only lasted a year. After we split up he met another woman and went to live with her, and when that wore thin for him he phoned and asked me if he could come back, but I said no.

During our short time together he had bought me a watch. I had never worn it, then one Saturday night when I was getting ready to meet my friend Doreen I noticed that my usual watch had stopped, so I had to wear the one he had given me.

Doreen and I were in the queue for the club we were going to when a man behind me told me that my watch had stopped at 7 p.m. Straightaway I knew it was a message from my ex and that he was dead.

When I got home I phoned around, but couldn't find out anything. Two days went by and I tried to forget about it. I decided to go out for the day to my sister's. I stopped halfway there and went into a shop I'd never been in before. Squeezing past two women who were talking, I heard one of them mention Stan – my ex's name – and how he had been out jogging on Saturday night and died at around 7 p.m. in the street.

When I got to my sister's house she told me that Stan's death had been in the paper. I really felt as if he had wanted to send a message to me that I had been right about his jogging.

It does seem from reading Charlotte's story that in death her ex was trying to tell his former wife that he regretted letting her down and not listening to her advice.

Every grieving person who has lost someone dear to them must wish that their lost loved one could still communicate with them in some way. It may sound like an impossible dream, but from my personal experience and from the vast number of letters I have received reporting this experience, it is a reality. Many people have written to tell me that they feel closer than ever to loved ones who have passed away. They talk of grief, but alongside it there is also comfort, warmth and feelings of overwhelming love.

After the terrible loss of her beloved son one lady wrote the following to me:

## A Warm and Deep Love

In April 2006 we lost our only child, a son. He was only 16 years old and died in a tragic accident when he was trying to help a friend. Since his death I have had some amazing experiences of him being so close and being enveloped in such a warm deep love that sometimes I feel he is sitting on my shoulder.

Caeth has this incredible experience to share:

## Unbelievable Light

My mom's death had hit me hard, even though I had been expecting it and I had looked after Mom in my home. Some time afterwards, on an ordinary night no different from the rest, I was in my dining room and suddenly, from out of nowhere, there was an unbelievable light. In it I saw an angel. She had long golden hair and around her was a light that I cannot explain and cannot describe. How beautiful she was.

She embraced me and, man, can I tell you, the warmth, the love, the safety of that embrace was something unworldly. I long for the day that I can feel that way again. I wish my children could feel that absolute love and safety when I embrace them. It was angelic, if I may use the word.

Then, without a sound, she lifted me up and up. I'm terrified of heights, by the way, but I felt so warm and safe and loved that it did not cross my mind to be scared. She held me close and we just went up and up. I know it sounds silly, but we went through the ceiling without feeling anything. I was as light as a feather. No words, no sound, just the embrace and the lifting up and up and up …

I awoke on my bed, remembering the wonderful experience. Thinking of it makes me emotional to this day. It was the most amazing experience of my life.

In that case it was an angel in traditional form who came to offer comfort, but sometimes those who have passed on will return to watch over those they have loved. Janet wrote to me to say that she believes her dad in spirit remains close to her. She and her daughter and mother actually believe they once saw him.

## 'As Plain as Day'

As I looked towards the kitchen, which has a half-door, there, as plain as day, was my dad walking past. I must admit I was very shocked. It was definitely him. He looked into the room right at me.

Carrie also realized someone she loved remained close to her after death:

## 'Lift Me Up'

When you've spent 28 years with someone they almost become a part of you. It's been five years since I lost Jack, my husband, and I miss him beyond belief, but a while back something happened that made me think that he wasn't far away at all.

I'm not as young as I used to be – I'll be 77 next year – and I went through a patch of having really nasty falls recently. I'd just be walking along and suddenly would keel right over. Mercifully it always happened when there were other people around and there was always some kind person to help me up, but then one evening as I was walking home from my local shop it happened again and this time there was no one there. I saw a couple of kids pass by on a motorbike, but I don't think they saw me, or if they did they probably thought I was drunk.

Then the most amazing thing happened and I still can't quite believe it. I smelled Jack's aftershave and then I felt a pair of strong arms wrap around my waist and lift me up in the air. I think I hovered there for a while and then I was gently set down on my feet. I looked around, but couldn't see anything or anyone. I knew it was Jack who had come to help me, though, as I felt him all around me and I still do. As I said, when you've spent that long with someone they become a part of you.

When her beloved son Terry died, Doris also felt as though the colour had drained out of her life, but then something extraordinary happened to lift her up.

## 'Arms All Around Me'

I am an 83-year-old lady and 13 months ago I lost my darling son. He took his own life after his marriage fell apart. He was in a mental hospital after having a breakdown and was on so many tablets he did not know one day from the next. He was so precious to us and I miss him every hour of every day.

After about six months of grieving, one day I was sitting in my armchair in front of a window. I was ill at the time. I broke down crying and asked my son to help me. After a few moments there was such a wonderful and serene feeling and an angel with large white wings came through the lounge window to my chair. I felt arms all around me, holding me close and stroking my hair as my darling son used to do when he was a little boy, and I knew it was him. He kissed me and went out the same way.

I will never forget my angel. It was so serene and lovely. And I know my son is still with me and that he is sorry for what he did and loves us all very much.

When the pain of living becomes harder than the pain of dying and a person takes their own life, the consequences can be devastating for grieving relatives. Suicide is not something that our angels and our loved ones want for us, but for reasons unknown, some people need to cross to the other side to receive healing and to fully understand that hell is only something that we create in our minds when we don't believe we are worthy of love.

Returning to the theme of messages from beyond the grave, Vicky's story shows that sometimes our loved ones in spirit choose to speak to us through the eyes and hearts of other people:

## The Man in the Black Waistcoat

This happened while I was working as a waitress in a fish and chip restaurant. I got on well with all the staff there, especially my boss, Michelle. One evening I was cleaning the middle section of the shop when a gentleman appeared to be standing in the back of the shop where we prepared the chips, etc. At first I was startled, but he appeared to be a jolly, friendly old man. He was smiling and wore a beige top and black waistcoat. He had white hair and looked hale and hearty. I continued my work and when I looked back a few minutes later, he had gone.

Vicky went on to see the gent two or three more times and she asked Michelle if she knew who he was.

Michelle then handed me a photo and asked me if this was the man I'd seen. The photo was of an old gentleman wearing a beige top and black waistcoat, looking very frail. I instantly said, 'Yes, that looks like the gentleman I saw, but he appeared healthy and happy to me, whereas in this picture he seems poorly.'

I was very shocked when Michelle then said the gentleman was her dad and at the time the picture was taken he was dying of cancer and the following week would be the third anniversary of his death. She and her family were planning to visit the local park, where they had had a memorial bench placed for him, and she'd been unsure whether it was the right thing to do or not.

I thought about it and decided that coming to the fish and chip restaurant was his way of telling her he was happy with them visiting the park. After that memorial visit I never saw him again, but I think my experience helped Michelle a lot.

Donna believes that the angels sent the spirit of a long-lost child to offer her grandmother reassurance and healing:

## Little Marjorie

My nan and granddad had 12 children, but sadly one daughter, Marjorie, died at the age of six months. During that pregnancy my nan had had to have a tooth out by gas and she blamed herself when Marjorie was born blue. As the months progressed, she knew that there was something very wrong with her daughter, but the doctors did not agree until one day she was admitted to hospital, where she died. My nan blamed herself for that child's death for years.

In 1974 she had to have major surgery on her legs and in those days patients were admitted days before the surgery. So Nan was in bed when a little girl aged around six or seven came and sat at the foot of it. My nan said she was so beautiful, peaceful and happy and she climbed up on the bed and kissed her on the cheek and told her she loved her very much and that she should not blame herself for her death. She said it was meant to be and that she was waiting for her.

After that day my nan didn't blame herself for her child's death anymore. She believed her baby had come back as an angel to comfort her.

Sometimes departed loved ones can also offer us reassurance that they are close to us through dreams, as in this story sent to me by Julie:

## 'It Felt So Real'

Six months after losing my dad I had a dream that was so vivid I woke at 5.30 a.m. in tears. In the dream I was at my father's house, sitting in his chair. My daughter was with me. The phone rang and I answered and it was Dad's voice and in the background chapel music was playing. I told him how much I missed him and that I hadn't wanted him to go. He told me he missed me too. I also told him about his forthcoming great grandchild. Then I woke up. It felt so real and I'm glad I told him my news.

It seems there are many ways for angels to communicate their love for us. Ethan kindly sent me this e-mail a few weeks ago:

## 'Text Me'

The last thing my best mate Steve said to me when he sped off in his old banger of a car – it was a real pile of junk – was 'I'll text you'. It was the end of our first year at college together and we wouldn't be seeing each other until the following October. We'd got on really well all year. We were on the same course and supported the same football team. I hadn't been very happy about leaving home for the first time, but as soon as I'd got to know Steve I'd had a ball. The year had raced by.

I got a job in the summer and started to save up for a car of my own. After a few weeks I wondered if I should text my friend but then I remembered that he'd said he'd text me. So I left it and before I knew it I was getting ready for the new academic year. The day before I was due to leave home I finally got that text from Steve. It said: 'Sorry, mate, 4 not txting. C U around.'

When I arrived back at college I looked around for Steve, but couldn't find him anywhere. Then I got the bombshell: he was dead. He had died in a motorway pile-up two weeks after I had waved goodbye to him. That had been more than a month ago, so how come I'd got the text a day before the start of term? I got in touch with Steve's parents and they told me that his mobile had been crushed in the pile-up. It's a mystery and I'm hoping you can clear it up for me.

I e-mailed back to tell Ethan that to my mind it was no mystery. Perhaps a rational explanation is possible, though I don't know how, as I am no mobile expert, but there is the strong likelihood that Steve was communicating to his friend from beyond the grave. As mentioned throughout this book, there are countless ways for angels to touch our lives and our hearts, and one way that many people feel they have chosen is through the spirits of those they have loved and lost.

A rational explanation is also possible for the next two stories, but as we'll see in the next chapter, angels can also communicate their love and healing presence in the most ordinary of ways.

Claire sent me this story two years after her beloved gran died:

## Lilies and Pearls

My gran was everything to me and as I was her eldest granddaughter we shared a very special bond. She was never keen on lilies because she said they reminded her of funerals. I like them, though, and have a violin full of satin lilies above my stairs at home. These flowers are glued in place. One morning in the week between Gran's death and funeral I went downstairs and on the third stair up was one of these lilies just lying there. I knew it was a sign from Gran, as I had had the violin of flowers for ten years and never once had they fallen out. They haven't fallen out since either.

When Gran died, we were each given a pair of her pearl earrings. She was known for wearing pearl necklaces and earrings, so the earrings really reminded me of her. One of them had a dodgy back and was prone to falling out, so I rarely wore them. However, in December last year I wore them to work and lost one of them in the office. I went into panic mode and had everyone looking for it. No one could find it and I got very angry with myself for wearing them that day.

I work in someone's private property near my house and the next morning I called into my home and the lost earring was there on the kitchen floor about 700 yards from the office building. I had no idea how it got there but I did know then that my gran was trying to let me know she was still very much a part of my life.

Whenever Karen visits her dad's resting place something incredibly special reassures her that he is closer to her than ever:

## Swan Lake

I have a special place where I can go to be close to my dad. I can see him standing by the bridge with his bag of bread feeding the ducks and swans. Finally, and this is so poignant, the lake is full of ducks and Canada geese but there is only one swan. Apparently he is disabled. I spoke to the head gardener there and he remembered my dad and how he would come daily to feed the birds. I told him he adored swans and had an affinity with them. He could even hand feed them.

The gardener then asked me what my dad's name was and when I asked him why, he explained that they had just discovered that the swan was male, though before they had thought it was female. So the lone swan has now been given a new name, Harold, after my dad, and every time I go to see him, he will swim up to me, stare for a while then swim away. I know it may sound silly, but I get so much comfort thinking that this swan is my dad in some form. Like Dad, he is disabled and, again like Dad, he is safe and in a place where he is loved.

## Dying to Live

Many of us find it hard to talk about death or to think about the prospect of our own death or the death of a loved one, but from my own angelic encounters and from reading the stories of people who have lost loved ones and received reassuring signs or visions from the world of spirit I want to leave you here with the thought that perhaps death is not the end but the beginning. It is just another natural stage in our existence.

I used to find the saying that you start dying the moment you are born incredibly depressing, but now, with the insight that time and experience have given me, I've come to understand that dying is a part of living and is a perfectly reassuring and positive thing. If you think about it, every night when you fall asleep you 'die' when your consciousness leaves your physical body and travels to the world of spirit. In this way, every morning when you wake up you have moved one step closer to heaven. You are an angel in waiting.

And, finally, just as dying is a part of living, it could also be said that living is a part of dying. Many people who have stepped into the world of spirit report that they have never felt so alive as during their experience. Donna, who feels that the spirits of lost loved ones are close by her every day, wrote and told me about her grandfather's near-death experience:

## No Words Can Express It

My granddad had a massive heart attack and actually died. He said that he saw a beautiful light and went to it. All of his family who had passed were waiting to greet him. He said that he had never felt anything like it and actually did not believe there were words to express what he had witnessed that day. He spoke to his family on the other side and they said that they were not ready for him and that he had to return to his family on Earth. He said it was a difficult choice, as the feeling of love was overpowering, but he was sent back and never feared death after that.

All fear of death does seem to evaporate once a person has caught a glimpse of heaven. Richard says it far better than I can:

## Staying Alive

There was an amazingly bright light and all of a sudden I was in an absolutely beautiful place. The sky was so blue. The weather was so perfect. I was on a huge big open lawn. Every member of my family and all my friends who had died were there. Even my dogs were there. I felt calmer than at any time in my life. I have never felt so at peace or happy. And it was all so real.

Then my brother came over to me and hugged me and smiled and said it wasn't my time yet and all of a sudden I was awake and gasping for breath and surrounded by a whole lot of doctors and nurses.

Since then I have felt so much calmer and also so much more alive. Death doesn't scare me now. I know that I am not going to die when my body dies. And so, with this new living-in-the-moment-of-death awareness, I've been feeling that I'm flying and yet at the same time standing still. I have never felt so alive and so present.

Chapter 9

# Everyday Angels

'There are two ways to look at the world: as if
everything is a miracle or nothing is a miracle.'

**Albert Einstein**

In France centuries ago peasants had an interesting tradition. Instead of simply saying 'Hello' when they met each other they would say, 'Good day to you and your companion.' Although they couldn't see them, they thought that guardian angels deserved to be greeted too!

I hope that reading the stories in this book will have encouraged you to be more open to the possibility that something wonderful exists, even though you may not be able to see, hear, feel or touch it. The real question to ask yourself is can you be open to wonder? Even at the very darkest moments of your life, can you be open to the new possibilities that are always there? Can you be open to the idea that angels are watching over you? If you sincerely want to, you can find those angels and experience the love, magic and joy they bring to anything and anyone, however ordinary and everyday.

The more you look for angels in the world around you, the greater the possibility of recognizing their presence. Children naturally have the ability to seek magic in the ordinary, but the stories in this chapter were all sent to me by adults who discovered the ability to see the world around them once more through the eyes of a child.

## Walking with Angels

In my research it's been intriguing to discover just how many people interact with angels on a daily basis. Some of these people have encountered an angel – whether through an angelic intervention in a crisis or a near-death experience – and have then found it easier to detect the signs that show an angel is walking by. Others have not encountered an angel directly but have found that an inexplicable event in their daily lives has opened them up to the spiritual world and they have become more receptive to angelic presence as a result.

When confronted with the unexpected, we can either explain it away as chance or interpret it as meaningful and guided by angels. Since you are in control of what you believe, why not believe in a philosophy that gives you greater hope? Why not believe in the idea that things happen for a reason? Why not believe in magic? Why not believe that things are not always what they seem? Why not believe in angels?

In most of the accounts in this next section, meaningful 'coincidences' happened in the course of everyday life and who is to say they weren't the work of angels? For Elizabeth, a series of events just fell into place:

## Day Shift

Six years ago, though I had worked night shifts for the previous 17 years, on one particular weekend I was asked to do the day shift. I wasn't happy about it, but I agreed.

In the early hours of Sunday morning my husband woke me to say he didn't feel well and had pains in the side of his face. I called the doctor and was advised to call for an ambulance. The hospital wasn't far away, so I put my husband into the car and drove him there, as it would be quicker than waiting for an ambulance. By the time we arrived he had collapsed. It turned out he had had a heart attack. He had to be shocked twice and have an operation, but recovered fully. I can't help but think that if I had been on my usual night shift there would have been no one to help him.

On another occasion, also a Sunday morning, as I was leaving work it started to rain. My colleague offered me a lift home but I was meeting a friend, so declined. My colleague called about ten minutes later to say a tyre had blown out on her car and the passenger side had smashed into a wall. If I had been in that car I wouldn't be writing this letter today.

Incidents like these are often dismissed as coincidence, luck or chance, but when someone finds themselves at the centre of a series of coincidences they are often filled with a sense of awe and reminded that the world can be a magical place in which angels may be at work.

## Jim and Bob

One summer evening Cathy set out on a blind date. She didn't have much faith in it amounting to anything, but having agreed to it she felt she couldn't back out now. She had been told to look for a blue car and a driver called John who would be wearing a blue shirt. They were to meet at eight o'clock outside the local post office. At a couple of minutes to eight John arrived and Cathy was pleasantly surprised.

After a film and before dinner John asked Cathy how she knew Bob. But she didn't know Bob. John was puzzled, because it was Bob who had set up the blind date for him. Cathy was confused then, as Jim had set up the date for her. But John didn't know who Jim was. After a few more whos and whats and what are you talking abouts, they realized that another couple must have made arrangements to meet at exactly the same time and place and they were out with the wrong date. Without hesitating, John told Cathy that he was having fun and wanted to continue. She agreed. Ten years later they are happily married with two sons, whom they decided to call Bob and Jim.

Believe it or not, this is a true story! And it shows that sometimes in life all we need to do is show up with an open mind and allow angels to do their work. If either Cathy or John had been rigid in their thinking, they might never have become a couple.

Paul got in touch to tell me about a series of meaningful coincidences that led him to his soul mate. I'll tell you his story:

## Susanna

Paul was a businessman who normally didn't believe anything without scientific proof but he had just had a wonderful experience that he believed could only be described as the workings of fate – or possibly angels. He had been in a stormy relationship for 18 months with a girl whom he cared for deeply but who had treated him badly. He suspected that she was only with him for his money. The relationship ended, as many do, with an argument over the phone. In frustration Paul destroyed his sim card so he would not contact her again and asked himself why he couldn't find someone who returned his love.

When he had calmed down he realized how daft it had been to destroy his sim card and placed an order for a new one on the internet. Three days passed and the sim card did not arrive, so he decided to buy one in the city instead. Just as he was about to leave his office he got an e-mail from the internet company saying that his order had been cancelled as the card he needed wasn't in stock. He called his service provider, who told him that if he went to a local shop he would be provided with a replacement card free of charge. In the shop he was served by a beautiful girl called Susanna. They fell in love and eventually got engaged.

Meaningful coincidences often seem to happen to bring two people into a relationship. In fact, when you consider the billions of people on the planet, isn't it a miracle that any of us find our soul mates?

For Nancy it wasn't a partner who was drawn to her by a startling series of coincidences, but members of her own family:

## Making Contact

Nancy wrote to tell me how after her mother's death she was looking through some of her photos and found some of a boy and girl she didn't know. She asked her aunt about them and she told her they were the children of her dad's first marriage. Her mum had never talked about them and Nancy wondered how she could get in touch with them. Then seven years later she found out through genes reunited that they were staying at the place she was heading towards with her caravan to see a show. She made contact with them there and they are still in touch today.

The chance meeting, the life-saving encounter, the lost object – or indeed relative – that suddenly reappears all seem to be the work of an unseen power and may well be signs of your guardian angel at work in your life.

I'm not sure if the next two stories tell us more about how angels work, but I'm including them here because the people who sent them to me were sincere in connecting events that might be described as fairly ordinary, or easy to explain rationally, to angels. Let's begin with Russell's account:

## 'The Force is with You'

It was the morning of my GCSE maths and I was feeling horribly anxious. I'd worked hard, but the previous year I'd missed quite a lot of school due to a serious chest infection. I'd done my best to catch up, but it had knocked my confidence quite badly. I wanted to go to university or college, so I needed to at least get a pass in maths. It wasn't my strongest subject, though, and I knew it and my teachers knew it.

Anyway, that morning as Mum cleared away the breakfast stuff I got a mini panic attack. I started to sweat and feel really sick. Mum felt my head and it was very hot. We were seriously considering ducking out of the exam when suddenly I heard, 'The force is with you, young Skywalker,' boom out from my *Star Wars* mug on the window sill, which had a battery-operated voice pack. We both burst out laughing and I instantly felt better.

I'd got that mug about six years before, when I was deep in my *Star Wars* phase. Every time you lifted it up it would say, 'The force is with you,' and play the *Star Wars* theme tune. I hadn't used it in years and it had just sat silently on my window sill. My mum said the sunlight must have triggered the speaker, but it had never happened before and I'm convinced it was my guardian angel who triggered it to give me a welcome bout of humour and self-belief.

Even better, Russell e-mailed me six months later to tell me that he had got the 'C' grade pass he needed.

Jane, too, believes that an angel was watching over her:

## Call Back

This happened 21 years ago now. I was excited about going away for a week-long vacation with my husband in Egypt. I'd never felt happier, as a few weeks before we'd agreed that the time was right for us to think about starting a family.

We'd ordered a cab to take us to the airport, but an hour or so before it was due to arrive the phone rang. A man said that he was very sorry but there was no way that a cab could get to us in time. I was furious and ranted down the phone, but it was no use. No other company could do it in time either. Reluctantly we decided to take our chances with the train. Fortunately we didn't miss our flight.

When we arrived back at the airport after a fabulous week, we got into a cab and asked to be taken home. It turned out that the cab was from the same company that had cancelled previously and I took the opportunity to have a rant. The cab driver said he had been the driver booked to collect us, but when he had arrived at our house there hadn't been anyone there. I couldn't understand that, because after all it had been the cab company that had cancelled the booking. But then the driver said something that sent shivers down our spines. He told us that it was a good thing we hadn't been collected by him because about 15 minutes afterwards, as he was on his way to his next job, one of his back tyres had blown, sending him crashing into a wall. He said that he had only suffered whiplash injuries, but the cab had been a write-off and it had been a mercy that no one had been in the back because they would probably not have survived.

When we got home there weren't any messages on my answerphone. Still thinking about what the cab driver had said, I did a call back, as it was highly likely that the last person to call had been that man from the cab company. The call-back service informed me that I had indeed been called on that day, but the number was unrecognized. So who had rung us to cancel that cab?

To this day Jane has no idea who the mysterious voice on the phone was or why her life and that of her husband were saved in that way, but, now the mother of four children, there's never a day when she doesn't feel grateful for it.

## Angels in Human Form

Sometimes in our daily lives we encounter angels and it is only when we reflect back that we recognize them for what they were. Nowhere is this truer than with angels who appear in human form. We've already talked about mysterious strangers who somehow appear at just the right time with the right kind of help, but it is such an everyday but special phenomenon I'd like to mention it again in connection with this story submitted to a *Sunday Post* readers' page and sent to me by Charlotte:

## The Angel Visiting Italy Island

While visiting the church on Italy Island I came across some children leaving notes on the board for loved ones who had passed on. A little girl asked me to pin her note up because she couldn't reach. She said thank you and explained the note was for her daddy.

'It's my birthday soon,' she explained, 'and he said he would buy me a special baby doll, but we've moved to a new house so I've sent him my new address.'

When she left the church I could not resist having a peep at her note and making a note of her birthday and her address. I bought her the sweetest doll I could find and sent it with a note explaining that because there were no shops in heaven I had done her daddy's shopping for him.

I signed my letter 'The lady who pinned your note on the board in the church on Italy Island'.

I love this charming story because yet again it shows there's potentially an angel in all of us. We can all be aspiring angels like the lady who visited the church on Italy Island, offering others simple gestures of love and helping them to feel that they have met an angel.

## Angelic Calling Cards

Angels can be found anywhere and everywhere, but one of the best-known signs that they are close by, as we've already seen, is a white feather.

Diana wrote to tell me how finding white feathers in places she wouldn't expect to find them has been be a huge comfort to her in the months following the death of her beloved daughter, especially as it was her daughter who taught her the significance of these feathers.

## A Beautiful Week

In October my partner and I were travelling to Suffolk for a week's caravan holiday. On the way we were waiting at traffic lights in a small Lincolnshire market town when a man crossed the road and told us there was water leaking from the front of the car. Fearing it was the radiator, we pulled up in the first available layby and my partner went to the front of the car. He bent down and there on the radiator grille was a white angel's feather which he handed to me. There was no sign of water leaking from the engine, so we assumed that the windscreen washer bottle had been overfilled. I burst into tears because I felt my daughter was with us, saying that it was right to go on this holiday. And it did turn out to be a beautiful week.

Another woman who felt comforted when she found a white feather was Celia:

## A Feather on the Doorstep

Celia had recently lost her beloved husband Brian to brain cancer and was heartbroken. Just before she found the white feather she had had a nasty fall but had been helped home by a kind man. She never saw the mysterious stranger again, but a white feather appeared on her doorstep as he said goodbye and the kindness of this stranger and the angel feather made her feel that she wasn't alone and that angels were supporting her through this difficult time in her life.

Sue Gulliver wrote to tell me that whenever she is stressed or worried about something or when an important decision needs to be made she finds a white feather and as soon as she sees one she knows with a calm certainty what do to. The feather incidents have fired her creativity and inspired her to write a poem about them, and here it is:

Have you ever seen a white feather lying in your
    path?
And wondered, 'Where did that come from?' and wryly
    laugh?
Did you think that a bird had dropped it or did you get
    a shiver?
Or did you think an archer had lost it from his quiver?

Just think when you next see a white feather on the
    ground,
'Am I being silly or has my Guardian Angel been
    around?'
If you've needed guidance or help in any way,
Has your problem been solved or eased at the end of
    the day?

I believe in angels and ask them all the time,
To help me, my friends and family through the daily
    grind.

They are around you to give guidance and help you all
    they can,
So don't be afraid to ask them, 'cos they've been sent
    by the Main Man.

As well as feathers, angels may also leave items of value
for us to find. These are usually coins that turn up in
unusual places or lost items that mean a great deal. Here's
what happened to Charlotte:

## Pennies from Heaven

I got married in 1953 and had my first baby, Christine,
soon after. My husband was in the merchant navy at the
time. I was living in my parents' house and when my little
girl was one year old I got a place in a nursery for her so
I could get a job to boost my £3 a week navy allowance.

Things worked out for a year, but then Christine got a
very nasty infection in her mouth and needed hospital
treatment. That was the end of the nursery and my job, but
thankfully she recovered. I got the keys to our first flat
around the same time. I was very happy, but couldn't
work out how I was going to manage on £3 a week.

On the second day in our new flat Christine was playing with her toy shop and asked me to play with her. I
said I would, but I hadn't got any money. She said it was
fine because she would give me some. I smiled, thinking it

would be toy money, but when she opened her bag and said, 'How much do you want?' it was full of £1 notes – £65 in all!

I thought I was dreaming. I asked her where she had got it all from and she said she didn't know, it had just been there when she had opened her bag that morning. I never did find out where it had come from or how it had got there, but I used it to pay off some debts and for the first time in my life I opened a bank account.

Something similar happened to Mrs Clark, who sent me this story:

## Silver Coins

A long time ago when my three children were very young we were very hard up. We were living in a small council house and one day my husband Jim decided to have a go at tidying up the small garden. When he started digging in the corner, he dug up four half-crowns, which in those days was a lot of money. We were pleased. A few weeks later we couldn't believe it when he found more silver coins just when we needed them.

As well as money turning up unexpectedly, another commonly recognized angel calling card is a beautiful floral fragrance that seems to appear from nowhere. You may also get a feeling that someone is touching or kissing you very gently either on your arm or face. It's a very gentle, loving touch, like that of a loving parent, and is just to let you know that angels are there and that they care for you. Some people hear an angel speaking softly to them or, like Marceline and her husband in the story below, the voice of a departed loved one doing angelic work.

## A Gentle Nudge

We live in Cyprus and run a little business where we fit out newly purchased villas and apartments. One evening not long after my dad died we put a lot of things in our car ready to take down to a villa in the morning.

At around 3 a.m. that morning my husband woke up. He looked out of the dining-room window, which overlooks the drive where our car was parked, and noticed that the security lights were on, suggesting that someone or something was coming up the drive. Nobody was there, but he heard my dad's voice calling him by his surname. My dad was the only person to call him by his surname and not his first name.

When he told me about it later that morning, I immediately said, 'I think Dad was just giving you a gentle nudge to check on the car and possibly letting me know he was with us.'

Angel Babies

Other people, like Anne, hear loved ones calling through the voices of other people:

## 'Bye, See You Soon'

My father David died three months ago and I miss him so much. Before he died he asked me whether I thought his family was going to be waiting for him. I said I absolutely did. He took a few minutes to digest this answer and then said, 'I will wait for you when you die.' It was incredible for my dad to say something like this, as he was very afraid of dying. I did say to him, however, not to be in too much of a hurry, as I was happy to wait a while to see him. My dad was a great joker and we laughed about this.

Just before he died I asked him to send me a message when he arrived to let me know that he was OK and had made it safely to meet my mother, the rest of his family and God. Sometime later I think I got it.

I had drifted off into a semi-sleep one night when I heard a child outside in the corridor shouting to an adult, 'Bye, see you soon.' The adult then replied with the same, 'Bye, see you soon.' This exchange went on for a few minutes, with the child laughing more loudly each time. I listened and laughed and felt it was a message from Dad saying he was fine and was waiting for me. I know that time is all relative and 'soon' in his time is not 'soon' in our time and I know he was teasing me about what I'd said about being happy to wait a while to see him.

I fell into a deep sleep after this event and feel quiet and calm now, which is great considering how I have been feeling since his death.

Then there are those like Suzy, who believe an angel definitely spoke to them:

## 'We All Have a Guardian Angel'

I truly believe we all have a guardian angel. There's a whole book that could be written about my life but all you need to know at this point is that when I was aged nine my step-father started to abuse me. He took his chances when my mum was working night shifts. She was a nurse. Anyway one night after the most horrible abuse I fell into a painful and deep sleep and when I woke up I saw an angel. He seemed enormous but then I was only a child so he was probably about six feet tall. He was floating at the bottom of my bed. Then he spoke to me. He told me that I was beautiful and pure and that I shouldn't cry. I felt a happiness and calm that I had never known before. He also told me he would always be with me.

The abuse stopped two days later. It may have been something in the way my step-father looked at me, but suddenly it was as if my mother just knew something was going on. She asked me to tell her what was happening. I wasn't able to, but she knew all the same. I think an angel spoke to her as well. I never saw my step-father again after that night. Although the memory of what he did to me will never leave, I also have the memory of my guardian angel appearing to me, and the sense of calm, purity and love that gave me will last me a lifetime – and beyond.

Quite apart from messages from the world of spirit, there are many ways in which angels can make themselves known and bring comfort and reassurance. A cool breeze on your face when there is no window or door open can be the touch of an angel, and if you feel a flutter in your tummy this might just be your guardian angel talking to you through your gut instinct or intuition. An unexpected sense of emotional well-being, a feeling of being loved and cared for, is, I believe, also the work of your angel.

Many people have written to me to tell me that they have found themselves inexplicably drawn towards buying a newspaper or magazine they would not ordinarily buy and then finding that there is a story or report in it that is relevant to them. Others talk of hearing answers to their questions when they use the radio, television or internet, or seeing them on a sticker on a window, bus or cab, or in a message on someone's

T-shirt. Another fascinating way for angels to reveal themselves is by the appearance of a certain number, most commonly 11.

Many people have written to tell me that certain songs speak volumes to them when they 'just happen' to be playing on the radio at exactly the right time. Could this be a form of angelic communication? Joanne describes the phenomenon:

## 'You Raise Me Up'

My grandma passed away three years ago now after battling multiple myeloma. She was like my second mum and I still miss her terribly. In the limo on the way to the funeral everyone around me was talking, but I was so devastated I couldn't speak. I was just staring out of the window, tears streaming down my face. I had never known grief like it. In my head I was thinking, 'I love you Grandma, why did you have to go and leave us?' Then suddenly the song 'You Raise Me Up' started playing in my head over and over. It's not a song that specifically meant anything to me and my grandma, but somehow the words gave me some form of comfort.

For weeks after the funeral I couldn't stop crying. I was driving in my car one day, tears in my eyes, having what I called 'a grandma moment', and I put the radio on to try and give myself something else to think about so I could of her, in fact in the dream I was her, and I was so depressed, so unhappy, sad – oh, it was a terrible dream. I woke up and thought, 'I hope that was just a dream and not how she really feels.'

Later that morning, after the usual rush to get three little ones off to school, I heard a knock on my door. Amazingly, there on my doorstep was Alison. She had never visited me before. 'Could you look after the key for me,' she said, 'and give it to my children when they come home from school? I have left a note on the door to tell them where to come.'

'Of course I will,' I said, and then (because of the dream!), 'but first come in for a few minutes and have a coffee.'

She protested she didn't really have time, but I was insistent and brought her into the house.

'Alison, are you alright?' I said. 'Please tell me if something is wrong.'

With that she burst into tears and confessed she had found out her husband was having an affair and she had taken an overdose and was getting out of the house to die!

I called an ambulance and she went to hospital and had her stomach pumped.

It seems that Alison's guardian angel was watching over her and was determined to alert someone to her plight.

remember angels don't restrict themselves to feathers, dreams, numbers or T-shirt slogans. If you know how to look for them you can find them anywhere and every-where, from flowers to rainbows, from hugs to clouds, from sunshine to rain and from every act of kindness to every positive thought. The presence of angels can be felt in every atom of creation. They are part of the intercon-nection behind all things visible and invisible which only those with the heart of a child can see.

## Forever a Child ...

Children know instinctively how to see the wonder in everything and they can teach us a great deal about find-ing the angels in our own lives. Sadly, there is so much pressure on children to be grown up today and to leave their childhood games and pleasures behind. Of course we all need to be responsible and independent and to treat others with respect, but if we feel like singing, skip-ping, playing, dancing, laughing, crying, letting our hair down or dreaming during the day and the night we should not put the brakes on. You are only as old as you think you are. As long as you remain passionate, sponta-neous, loving and in the moment, you will forever remain a child in the eyes of angels.

One of the greatest gifts my belief in angels has given me is the gift of my childhood. As you may have gathered, I was a rather serious and anxious child, old before I was young. I tried to control every aspect of my life, thinking that was the way forward, but when I got older and learned to relax and let go of fear and self-doubt I slowly began to realize that feeling truly alive is about expecting the unexpected and living fully in the present moment. With this new understanding, my heart and mind opened to angels at last, and love, laughter and the magic of childhood flooded back into my life.

To invite angels into your life you don't need to conduct a formal invocation ceremony or to study and train or go on fasts and retreats, all you need to do is go beyond your fear and open up a two-way conversation with the unseen forces of the universe. If you reach out in this way with an open and trusting heart and mind, your guardian angel will be there to hold your hand and guide you, as a loving parent guides a child, through the challenges, possibilities and wonders awaiting you in this life and the next.

Living with angels will not always be easy – if life were always easy we would never learn and grow – but challenges and setbacks do become so much easier to bear when you understand that you are never alone and your angels are always with you, however lost, alone and afraid you may feel. They are there to show you your own possibilities and to remind you of everything that is wonderful about living.

So try to open your heart and mind to the angels around you and within you and to think positively about yourself and others so that you can help both yourself and others to have self-belief and the will to love. In this way you will be helping to bring angels closer to Earth. And when the time comes for you to cross over to the other side, not only will you have left the world a brighter and better place but you will be flying without fear and regret towards your new home in spirit, a home some people like to call heaven. Whatever name you choose to use, it's a place where peace and love reign and angels sing.

## Calling All Angels

And now as this book draws to a close I'd like to invite you to share some of your inspiring angel experiences with me. (You'll find details of how to do this on the following page.) Who knows, they might appear in a future book. The more we share stories of love and magical possibility, the more we attract love, magic, laughter and angels into our lives.

We all have an angel story within us, it's just that many of us never realize what that truly means. Remember, angels can come to us in countless different ways and even if we aren't quite sure they exist, they don't disappear. Children are naturally close to them, but we all have guardian angels watching over us and waiting for the moment when we find the courage to let our inner angel out to play. And when we do that, miracles begin to happen all around us.

Everyone has an angel story. What's yours?